DOCKERS' STORIES
FROM THE SECOND WORLD WAR

DOCKERS' STORIES
FROM THE SECOND WORLD WAR

HENRY T. BRADFORD

The
History
Press

Frontispiece: A Thames sailing barge and motor cargo vessel. (Author's collection)

First published 2011

The History Press
The Mill, Brimscombe Port
Stroud, Gloucestershire, GL5 2QG
www.thehistorypress.co.uk

© Henry T. Bradford, 2011

British Library Cataloguing in Publication Data.
A catalogue record for this book is available from the British Library.

ISBN 978 0 7524 5688 1

Typesetting and origination by The History Press
Printed in Great Britain

CONTENTS

Lorries waiting to offload freight for export, London Docks. (Author's collection)

ACKNOWLEDGEMENTS

I am greatly indebted to John N. Black, the former chief executive and deputy chairman of the Port of London, for his perseverance with the reading of these tales of dockers and stevedores, Freemen of the Company of Watermen and Lightermen, the tugboat crews of the River Thames and the docklands, all of whom formed the workforce that operated the Port of London, from Teddington Lock to Sea Reach, where the Thames estuary joins the North Sea between Havengore Creek, in south Essex, and Wardens Point, in north-east Kent. Further I must thank him for those corrections he advised in relation to 'times, tides and other subject matter' while reading these tales, and whose constructive advice I very much appreciated during the revision. Then I offer my thanks to:

Mrs Valerie Thomas for the information relating to her father's First World War French medal and the photograph of her late father.

Mrs Daphne Trott for her permission to publish her late husband's photograph and his naval parchment, the record of his naval service. (Leslie was one of the three men discussing the loss of convoy PQ17 in Tale 1.)

Mrs Joyce Smith for the loan of her papers, relating to her late husband's involvement in the 13th Battalion Parachute Regiment, 6th Airborne Division's so-called Malayan Mutiny, and for allowing the use of photographs of Ernest (Ernie) during his wartime military service.

Albert Fryer, the last of the fourteen-year-old boy seamen to receive his Second World War medals, for taking the time to accompany me to the National Archives at Kew to study his father's wartime tug log books. Also his sister Mrs Sylvia Wakeman for the loan of their father's scrapbook and medals, a document and awards that show the strong character of a man dedicated to a very dangerous occupation and showing too the calibre of the 'civilian tugboat crews' that served with him.

To my niece, Mrs Diana Newman *née* Fuller, for the photographs of her parents and her father's framed citation of his 'Mentioned in Dispatches'.

Next to my friend Philip Connolly, the conservator of all my writings, whose advice I am often bound to seek in the use of electronic gadgetry, together with that of Derek and Marion Cooper who came to my aid when Philip fell ill.

Then, too, I have especially to thank my late former workmates in the port transport industry, without whose experiences inside the docks, in their previous occupations, and their wartime

The author, Henry T. Bradford. (Author's collection)

military experiences in near and far away lands, these tales of heroism, and in Ernie Smith's case demeaning incarceration in a military rison, could never have been written.

I shall always have to be thankful to the late D.J. Foley, MBE, JP, my mentor and friend, the former welfare officer at Sector 3 Office, London Dock Labour Board, Tilbury Docks. For without Dan's persistence in my further education, and my tutor Professor Keith Thurley of the London School of Economics and Political Science, these tales of the London docklands, of the rivers Thames and Tyne, could never have been written.

Finally, to the Revd Peter Duncan, padre to the Port of London, with whom I worked on a number of projects intended for the benefit of the Registered Dock Workers of the Docklands of the Port of London.

I thank you, one and all.

Henry T. Bradford

INTRODUCTION

MR DUNLOP — THE EIGHTH MAN

There are here eight tales of the bravery and escapades of men (including Mr John Dunlop) who, once the wars they had fought in were over, returned to work in the docklands of the Port of London, on the River Thames, in sailing barges, or on coastal or continental short-sea trading vessels. Of course, there are so many other tales of a similar nature that could be told, were there enough space here for me to write about them.

These eight tales are about four men who received military awards for bravery (Tales 2, 6, 7 and this introduction) and four men who did not (Tales 1, 3, 4, 5). However, there are numerous other tales that could be told of the thousands of other men employed in the port transport industry alone who deserved awards, but whose courage in difficult circumstances went unnoticed or unrecognised. To them I make my sincerest apologies.

Obviously I was not myself a participating belligerent during the Second World War, but a passive child who, with many thousands of other children, was evacuated away from my home. But this did not preclude us members of the civilian population from being embroiled in the war and experiencing the wonders of modern warfare through enemy bombing of our cities, towns and villages. But at least that experience gave me some little insight into the traumas that the men whose stories I have narrated must have felt during their enforced preoccupation during battles with the enemies of the State.

I must point out too that it was my experience that the men who were caught up in the worst fighting, and who suffered the most from their wartime experiences, were the hardest nuts to crack when one was trying to extort information from them. In other words, the worse the experience, the least said. Now take for example the case of John Dunlop, who was the Port of London Authority's foreman for Tilbury Docks' riverside deep-water jetty. John Dunlop was one of those quiet men. He rode about his allotted area of responsibility in the docks on a bicycle. The reason for this was the riverside deep-water jetty was a concrete island jutting out into the river, just below the New Lock entrance. The only practical way of covering the long distance between the Port Authority's southern docks office and the jetty catwalk was by cycling, which incidentally was an offence under Port Authority bylaws with a fine levied on offenders.

However, it was long after John Dunlop retired from the Port of London, in fact it was on his golden wedding anniversary, that his story of courage under enemy fire came to light. Then he told in his own simple words how the incident occurred for which he was awarded the Croix de Guerre with Palm. He said:

John Dunlop, Croix de Guerre with Palm, in Civil Defence uniform during the Second World War. (Author's collection)

I was a dispatch rider and was sent to collect some mail. On my way back I went to look for a friend who I understood was in one of the trenches, but I lost my way and went behind the French lines without realising it. I saw a staff car that had overturned and no one was trying to help the two injured French officers inside. I knew now I was behind the German lines, but I drove to the car and helped the two French officers into my sidecar. I was being fired at all the time, but luckily not hit. Back at French headquarters I refused to give my name because I should possibly have been brought before a Court Martial for disobeying orders. So a senior French officer presented me with the Croix de Guerre with Palm. I was afraid to tell anyone at first in case I landed myself in trouble; then it wasn't worth telling anyone.

That then is the calibre of men these tales are about: extraordinary, ordinary, common men.

TALE 1

THREE FORMER ROYAL NAVY SEAMEN DISCUSSING THE LOSS OF RUSSIAN CONVOY PQ17

It was lunchtime on an extremely cold December day. I had climbed out of the freezing cabin of the 80ft jibbed Stothert & Pitt electric crane I had been driving, clambered down its steel rungs, whose cold metal tried to arrest each of my hands on its icy bars, on to the quayside. The ship's quay gang was clearing the last chests of tea from the landing pitch into the transit shed, from alongside the Clan-Line cargo ship we were discharging, ready to make a quick start when we commenced work after lunch.

The winch drivers, who had been working steam winches at other holds on the ship, and their top-hands, had already gone ashore. The ship's down-hold gangs were popping up out of the deck booby hatchways one at a time, as slowly as air bubbles rise through a glass of newly poured Drambuie, and just as slowly they made their way to the Port Authority's canteen, to 're-fuel' on subsidised lunches and relax their tired muscles before they returned to the ship to slog their way through the rest of the day. A journey of hard labour that was to last them till they retired, were injured or died of old age, if they should be so lucky.

Those of us who had less arduous and physically demanding jobs, and were saving up to get married or trying to make ends meet for numerous purposes (such as cost of living expenses, mortgage repayments and family holidays), would gather in the Port of London Authority's gear shed, which was a sanctuary within the docks. It was a place where we could take our pre-packed sandwiches and get a cheap cup of tea made for us by the gear storekeeper, who acquired the tea from damaged chests taken for repair to the coopers and box-knockers' workshops in one of the transit sheds. It was the only way the storekeeper could earn an addition income to supplement his paltry weekly wage. In the gear store we would sit by a warm coke-fired combustion stove and snooze our lunch hour away, drugged by the fumes from the coke, or talk or just listen to the tales of the older men, whose lives had been spent either in the service of their king and country, fighting wars in distant lands, or on the high seas as Royal Navy or Merchant Seamen, long before they became wage slaves in the port transport industry.

Ship's crewmen, HMS *Collingwood*, 1942. Able Seaman Leslie Trott is second right in the back row. (By kind permission of Mrs Trott)

The tales they discussed between themselves always fascinated me, simply because they were told in that reserved British manner of those days. That is, as though what they had done, the ordeals they had gone through in battles during wars, in countries the world over, the families and comrades they had lost, were all just part of a macabre game. Sometimes, when one of these military or civilian veterans got angry at some offensive remark made by one or other of his contemporaries, he would raise a finger menacingly. Then, on regaining his placidity, he'd smile and clam up; or, if he was incensed or offended by the remark, battle would commence – blood would be spilled.

There was an occasion when three of the men, former Royal Navy deck ratings, were talking between themselves in subdued voices about a convoy they had been escorting to Russia during the Second World War. One of the other dockers, who had been with General Montgomery's 8th Army in the western desert, butted in on their conversation with some ludicrous remark about the navy, to which he received the 'stiff finger' in his treatment, then the smile, then the verbal retort: 'You should have been there with us on those Arctic convoys. Do you know, once we ran out of butter, and had to do with spreading margarine on our bread. I ask you, margarine.' That's the sort of men they were.

What they had been talking about, which was meant to be a discussion between themselves, in low voices that were just above whispers, was the ill-fated Russian convoy PQ17. All three of them had been with convoy PQ17 in July 1942, in cruisers that had been ordered by the First Sea Lord, Sir Dudley Pound, together with all other Royal Navy surface ships, to withdraw from protecting convoy PQ17, because the Admiralty in London had been misinformed that a German pocket battleship had put to sea.

2.

Name *TROTT Albert Leslie*

Name of Ship. (Tenders to be inserted in brackets)	Substantive Rating	Non-Substantive Rating	From	To	Cause of Discharge and other notations authorised by Article 606, Clause 9, K.R. and A.I.
Collingwood	Ord. Sea		14 Apl. 1942	14 July 42	
Pembroke			15 July 42	9 Sep. 42	
Marlborough	A.B		10 Sep. 42	13 Apl. 43	
" "	A – B.		14 Apl. 43 1 March '43	17 Dec. 43	AFO. 3250/42
Pembroke			18 Dec. 43	2 Inch. 44	
		S.T.	3 Inch. 44	15 Mch. 44	
Bellona	A.B		16 March '44	21 Dec. 44	
" "	A/Leg.Sea (54)		22 Dec. 44	15 May '46	
Pembroke			16 May '46	1 Aug. 46	Released Class A. SP 391.

Royal Naval parchment – Record of Service – for Able Seaman Leslie Trott. (Author's collection)

The convoy had then been ordered to disperse, and the merchant ships were to make their own way independently to Russian seaports. The consequence of that order by the Admiralty in London, to abandon convoy PQ17, was that over the next few days of July 1942 German U-boats, E-boats and Luftwaffe aircraft between them sunk twenty-six of those unarmed merchant ships – ships that were carrying hundreds of crated aircraft, tanks, lorries, and tens of thousands of tons of stores and ammunition worth hundreds of millions of pounds, as aid to the Russian war effort.

In the next few days after that order was given, the Germans had been allowed a free hand to destroy the work of many months in British factories, and to take the lives of hundreds of merchant seamen (unarmed civilian non-combatants). It was one of the most disgraceful and dishonourable acts ever perpetrated on one's own countrymen, by a high-ranking officer of the king's navy; and to have listened to the former Royal Naval seamen, anyone would have thought it was their decision that caused the catastrophe. All those years after that disastrous event, the shame and guilt of it was still on their consciences, and would be until the day they died.

'Taking notice of the Admiralty in London showed a real lack of initiative,' one of them said. 'The Admiralty order to Commander Brome and Rear-Admiral Hamilton should have been ignored by them.' Commander Brome and Rear-Admiral Hamilton were the Merchant Navy convoy controller and the naval fleet commanders. 'Nelson wouldn't have stood for it,' one of them said. 'It would have been the telescope to his blind eye and: "I see no enemy ships, sail on."'

'Damn right it would have been,' replied one of his mates, 'at least those poor bloody merchant seamen would have had some chance in a protected convoy. Without us they had no chance at all, the poor sots. The senior officers were afraid to use their own initiative; afraid of the consequences if they'd been wrong and gone on protecting the convoy. That was the problem. They'd lost the Nelson touch.'

(See *The Guinness Book of Naval Blunders*, by Geoffrey Regan.)

TALE 2

THE ADVENTURES OF TWO JACK TARS IN A BOAT, WITH A WREN

'Well mates, that naval commander and rear-admiral should have been with me during the war,' interjected Jack, 'then they would have learnt what initiative was all about.'

Jack was much older than most of the other men sitting round the combustion stove. He had volunteered for wartime service with the Royal Navy in January 1940, when he was thirty-seven years of age, although you would never have guessed his age. Jack was a Freeman-Waterman-Lighterman of the River Thames. Jack knew every inch of the river and its foreshores, from Teddington Lock to the Nore, the Maplin Sands and beyond. As a boy from the age of twelve (working-class children left school at this age, until the introduction of the Fisher Education Act 1918, an Education Act that established compulsory education in England and Wales for children up to the age of fourteen), Jack started work sailing as the 'mate' on Thames barges, sailing craft that plied their trade on the River Thames, round the coast and even across the English Channel to ports in Belgium and France. That experience ended when he was 'apprenticed' to his father to become a Freeman-Waterman-Lighterman of the River Thames, where his days were taken up on the river, or in the locks and docks of the Port of London, looking after Thames lighters.

'How come, Jack? What happened to you?' he was asked:

Well, it was like this. I hadn't been in the Royal Navy very long. I'd just finished my initial training, in fact. I'd been detailed to report to Chatham naval barracks. It was mid-May 1940, and the weather was absolutely beautiful, with long sunny days and star-lit nights. Nobody in this country really knew that bloody battles were raging between British and German troops in Belgium and France, just thirty or forty miles away across the English Channel. For my part, I'd been settled in Drake barrack block, and on the following day, at first light, I was woken up by a Royal Marine bugler sounding reveille, at some unearthly hour it seemed, but in fact it was 5a.m. I'd got dressed on the double, and with the rest of the jack tars in my block, we tumbled out of the barrack block like children tumbling out of school, on to the parade ground, where a chief petty officer was waiting with tolerable patience, for a Royal Navy petty officer that is, encouraging us to assemble with endearing words such as: 'Come on you idle bastards, get fell in, you're slower than a gay bridegroom getting ready for bed with your newly wedded lady bride,' and other endearing comments that even you hard-nosed lot of sots shouldn't be made privy to.

'We've all been there and done that Jack, but what happened when you were assembled on the parade ground?' he was asked.

'Don't be so damn impatient, I'm coming to that,' he said, as he took a swig from his mug of tea before continuing his story:

When the chief petty officer had us standing to attention he strolled up and down our ranks a few times, prodding some of us in the belly and others in the arse with his swagger stick, just to let us know who was boss. He walked out to face the assembled parade before barking out: 'If there is any seaman here who knows anything about the River Thames, step forward.'

Now I thought that order was a bit iffy, verging on the suspicious, especially because Chatham Royal Naval barracks is sited beside the River Medway, but he did say the River Thames, so I took a chance and stepped forward out of the line.

The petty officer walked up to me, looked me up and down, walked round me as though he'd never seen a specimen like me before, then, pushing his nose almost into my ear, 'So, sailor boy! What do *you* think you know about the River Thames?' he roared out like a bull elephant.

'Everything,' I replied in a loud clear voice, loud enough for all my shipmates on parade to hear.

Then the loud-mouthed sot burst out laughing, spraying me with spittle before he repeated, 'Everything?'

'Yes, everything,' I replied. He was on my territory now.

'So how does it come about that one of His Majesty's jolly jack tars knows everything about the River Thames?' he bellowed for the benefit of the assembled parade.

'Because,' I told him in as loud a voice as I could muster, without him being able to charge me with insolence, 'I'm a Freeman-Waterman-Lighterman of the Thames.'

'And what might that elongated title mean, sailor?' he again bellowed in my ear.

'Well, what it means is, if we were on a craft on the River Thames, either I or a river pilot, or some other Freeman-Waterman-Lighterman would have to be in charge of piloting the craft.' I just left him with his own tiny biased mind to try working it out.

'What?' he yelled out. 'You in command of ships?' Then he scowled at me and said, 'Wait here.' He turned back to face the sailors and after a few 'attentions' and 'at eases' to relieve his pent-up frustration, he dismissed the parade. 'Follow me,' he growled. I did as I was bid, and he led me from the parade ground to the admiral's administration offices.

It was not long before the chief petty officer and I were asked by a stern-faced but pretty-looking WREN petty officer to 'follow me'. We were led into an inner office, where a tired-looking young man, white haired and old beyond his years, dressed in a first lieutenant's uniform, was seated at a beautiful antique desk that had possibly been there since the naval barracks had been built, a couple of hundred years before.

'Name and number?' he asked in a voice as tired as he looked old.

'Hicks, sir,' I replied, and gave him my ratings number.

'Know something about the River Thames, do you Hicks?'

'I'm a Freeman-Waterman-Lighterman of the Thames, sir.'

'A Freeman of the Thames! My God! What luck!' he blurted out. 'Then you're just the man I'm looking for. I've got a job for you, Hicks. Wait outside.'

We saluted, the CPO and me, about-turned and marched out of the office and waited, in my case to find out what orders I was to be given. I didn't have to wait long, just a few minutes. Then the WREN petty officer came out with a sealed envelope on which was written something like: 'Sealed orders: *To be opened only when on board LB13.*'

There was also a second opened letter that gave me the substantive rank of acting petty officer and advised me in which port I would find my boat. It also gave me orders to the effect that 'the boat' was to be stored up ready for sea on my arrival at the designated port – dockets to draw stores were enclosed with travel warrants – and that I should give due diligence to speedily getting the boat round to the River Thames as quickly as possible. The orders also gave me the power to commandeer anything I may need to expedite my mission, and informed '*Who or whomsoever this may concern*' Petty Officer (Acting) 34345 Hicks J. is in command of LB13 en route from Rosyth on the Firth of Forth to Tilbury Passenger Landing Stage on the River Thames.

After having read my orders, I passed the letter to the CPO, just to deflate that ignorant, arrogant, loud-mouthed, bullying bastard's power-inflated ego. Then, having taken the letter from his hands which were trembling with rage, and to the WREN petty officer's 'good luck', I made my way quickly back to Drake barrack block to collect my personal kit, before heading north to take command of my first Royal Navy boat, LB13.

I was stopped twice by crushers, Royal Naval Military Police patrols, on my walk from Chatham naval barracks to Rochester railway station, but I was quickly allowed to proceed on my way once I had shown the coxswains in charge of each patrol my letter of authority. I caught a Southern Railway electric train at Rochester railway station, which took me to London Bridge station; from there I got a taxi to King's Cross station to catch a steam train for the long journey north to Scotland.

Being cooped up in a third-class carriage was tedious, though. The carriages and corridors were packed to capacity with servicemen up to the rank of sergeant, or in my case petty officer (acting unpaid). I thought at the time: *I should be in a first-class carriage with the officers – after all, I am to be the captain of one of his Britannic Majesty's LBs.*

'Where did you have to go to pick up this boat you were to be in command of, Jack?' one of the men asked.

'Rosyth,' Jack replied.

'Where's Rosyth?' asked the docker who had made the derogatory remark about the navy.

If you'd been in the navy, and not the army, you would have known that. There can't be a sailor who's served in the Royal Navy that didn't know where Rosyth is. It's on the Firth of Forth, upriver on the northern shore opposite to that of Edinburgh. Anyhow, I'd never been to Rosyth myself. Then, when I did arrive at the naval base there to report, the duty officer perused my letter of authority and, ordering me without any further ado to 'Follow me, Hicks', he led me from his office to a quay, where a battered old wooden boat lay, gently rolling back and forth with the tide, rubbing itself against the dock wall, like an old cow scratching itself against a five-barred gate in a countryside meadow.

'There she is, Hicks, your command. She's just been requisitioned for a hush-hush job somewhere. She's stored up and ready to sail. As you can see, she's a clinker-built job, about thirty or forty years old, I'd say. She's 40ft from stem to stern and 12ft across her beam. She's a flat-bottomed craft, probably built for inland waterways, river or close in shore work. She's got a shallow retractable centreboard that should give her a bit of stability when you get to sea. Your crew are already aboard and raring to get under way. As I said, the boat has been stored up. You had better give me the stores dockets for them. Then you can cast off as soon as you've got yourself installed.'

He then passed me a bundle of papers, a pair of binoculars, some North Sea coastal charts, a compass, a tide table and a canvas bag with a heavy weight in it. 'Just in case you should come into contact with any of the Boche, put your maps and charts in the bag and throw it overboard,' he ordered. 'By the way, Hicks, that old girl [he was referring to the boat, of course] tends to roll about like a nymphomaniac in bed with a sexually frustrated drunken sailor. That broad beam, her shallow draught and, with a shallow retractable centreboard, she turned turtle [capsized] once so I understand. A couple of her crew were drowned. So if I were you, old man, I'd put half a ton of ballast below decks, port, starboard and mid-ships, before I cast off. That should put her down in the water and keep her a bit more stable. By the way,' he said it casually, 'we're short of men so we've had to draft an extra body in to make up the crew, good luck.' He then turned and walked away, and I was left alone to deal with my own problem of getting HMS LB13 from Rosyth, on the Firth of Forth, to Tilbury Passenger Landing Stage on the Thames, without turning her bottom up.

When the lieutenant had left I clambered down from the quayside's steel ladder, with my kitbag slung over my shoulder and my papers tucked under my arm. I stepped aboard LB13 and slid back the door to the deck cabin that was also its chart room and bridge-house, where I beheld what I thought were two Royal Navy seamen, sitting at the chart table, each with a mug of tea in his hand. When they turned toward me I could see the surprise register in their eyes, as they looked at me in my seaman's uniform; but their surprise wasn't as great as mine. For one of the seamen wasn't – it was a young woman dressed in a matelot's uniform – a beautiful, round-faced redhead with greyish blue eyes. I was greeted by the seaman with a churlish, 'And what can we do for you, mate?'

'Well,' I said it with the stern authority I'd already learned from naval petty officers, 'as you come to ask. One of you can get me a mug of tea to start with, milk with two spoonfuls of sugar. Then when I've drunk that, we will all go ashore and find some heavy lumps of flat scrap metal plate. Anything will do that we can lay over the lower deck cabin floor mid-ships, and the engine room floor. We need it to act as ballast to put this old cow down in the water a bit deeper, just to stop her rolling over when we get her out in the North Sea. By the way, I'd better introduce myself. I'm not your mate, mates. I'm your skipper for this trip. Jack Hicks – acting petty officer. Right, so – now who are you two?'

'Smith, sir; ordinary seaman Tom Smith. I've been sent here as the acting engineer,' the first one said.

'And you?' I asked the other one, and added 'Don't call me sir.'

'I'm WREN Matilda Caruthers-Lipton. I'm here acting as deck crew. Shall I refer to you as skipper or skip?' she said with the cultured voice of a BBC newscaster.

'Well!' I exclaimed. 'With all the "acting this" and the "acting that" that I've got here, I think we should call this boat "HMS Rada", or "HMS Showboat", don't you?' Then, after a short pause to let the seriousness of our predicament sink in, I said, 'You had both better call me Skip for the duration of this trip. I'll call you Tom,' I told the engineer, 'and you Mattie, if you don't mind,' I told Matilda Caruthers-Lipton.

'Oh that's absolutely fine, Skip,' she said. 'That's what the girls at my public school always called me.'

'Really,' I said it without surprise, 'jolly hockey sticks then, wizard prang old girl,' mimicking a slang comment I'd heard an RAF sergeant pilot say to his friend on the train when I was on my way to Rosyth from London. Mattie smiled, poured me a mug of tea and, ignoring my remark, sat and watched as I sipped it while seated at the chart table.

'Haven't you got something better you could be doing?' I asked her. I was beginning to feel a bit embarrassed.

She smiled at me again before replying, 'I don't want to disturb you while you're drinking your tea, Skip, but Tom and I are waiting on you for our orders.'

It was then I thought I'd better put them in the picture as to why I, a common ordinary seaman, was in charge of this boat, so I said: 'Before I open my sealed orders, I'd better tell you roughly why I'm in command of LB13. It's because, being as we are in the Royal Navy, it was thought this job was beneath the dignity of any regular officer or petty officer in the King's Senior Service, and as I'm technically a Merchant Navy man, and therefore I am assumed to know something about boats, and as the Royal Navy is scraping the bottom of the barrel for real seamen, I wasn't asked if I would mind doing them a favour and take charge of this old recovered wreck, I was ordered to.' Then: 'Right,' I told them, 'these are my sailing orders. [The orders I had received at Chatham read something like this, if my memory serves me correctly:]

'"Acting Petty Officer Hicks J., will take command of LB13 in Rosyth and sail her to Tilbury Landing Stage, on the River Thames, with due diligence and the utmost speed, but to take not longer that ten days after leaving Rosyth; the crew members shall each then report back to their home base for further orders on reaching the pier head at Southend,

By order of the Admiralty."'

'Okay. Now we'll all go ashore and purloin some heavy sheets of flat steel plate, and stow them below decks as close to the keelson as we can get it, and don't forget we must make sure it's secure: I don't want it sliding about when we get out to sea — it could cut our feet off. I'm going to chart a course out of the Firth of Forth into the North Sea. It looks to me as if the tide has about three hours to run on the ebb, and this is a slow-flowing river. So if we can get away in the next half-hour we could cross over to the south side of the river and lay up for the night in Leith, before we set off for the River Thames and Tilbury Riverside Passenger Landing Stage.'

It was then that Tom Smith, my boat's engineer, asked if he could have a private word with me.

Mrs Kay Bardoe, WREN, 1942. (By kind permission of Sidney and Kay Bardoe)

WREN Elmie Bardoe, 1942. (By kind permission of Kenneth Bardoe)

'Step ashore,' I ordered him. Then I asked, 'What is it?'

'To be quite honest it's like this, Skip. I don't know the first thing about boat engines. When we were on parade in Portsmouth Naval Barracks, the chief petty officer asked if anyone knew anything about engines, and I, like a village idiot, stepped forward. You see, I've got an Austin Seven motorcar which I maintain myself, that is I de-coke and reset the valves, replace the piston head gasket, change the sparking plugs and oil, and top up the water in the radiator and battery. I didn't know they wanted an engineer to run a boat's engine. Then, when I turned up here, I found the deck crew was a young woman who probably knows less about crewing a boat than I do about running a boat's engine.'

'Well now Tom,' I told him, 'don't worry too much on that score. I've got good news, bad news and indifferent news for you.'

'Oh, what's that?' he questioned with a deep frown.

'The good news is that I'm a Freeman of the River Thames. I know about barges, lighters and coasters, which is far more than can be said about your engineering capability. On the other hand, I don't know anything about the north-east coast of Britain, but if we ever manage to get down the coast as far as Colchester, I'll take you safely up the Thames to Tilbury Riverside Landing Stage whatever the weather or the state of the tides. The bad news is that if or when we get out of the Firth of Forth into the North Sea, I don't in all honesty know whether I have to turn left or right to get down the east coast into the River Thames.'

'My God!' he gasped, 'What have I let myself in for? What's the indifferent news?'

I burst out laughing and said, 'I wonder how our WREN deck crew got posted to this job?' And I left it at that.

By the time we had purloined a load of scrap steel plates and stowed them below decks, and made them secure to my liking, LB13 was down in the water by another foot. She had stopped rolling herself against the quay wall and now had a draft of about 6ft; she felt altogether more stable and seaworthy. However my only worry was that now we had a ton or two of steel aboard, it may attract the unwanted attention of a magnetic mine, but I kept that thought to myself for the time being.

As soon as we had finished our routine chores, I ordered Mattie, my crewman, to raise the White Ensign on the stern flagpole. I also gave her the order to cast off, hoping to God she knew what I was talking about – she did. I then set LB13 on course across the Firth of Forth, heading for our first port of call, Leith, where we tied up for the night while I set myself the task of plotting a course down the east coast of England for the River Thames.

When Tom and Mattie had turned in, I sat at the chart table working out my intended course south. I had very little idea how to navigate, so it was obvious to me I had to hug the coast. My main problem was to be sure of catching the tides and tidal streams, which rise and fall – ebb and flow. Of course, I had been issued with charts that showed the main off-shore shipping lanes, but I've got a simple mind that is operated by a minuscule brain. What's more, my seamanship was learnt through years of practical experience. So what, I thought, shall I do? Then an idea came to me.

I got up and went ashore, making my way to the nearest garage. There I purchased a *1939 Ordnance Survey Road Atlas of Great Britain*. The garage proprietor told me he was supposed to hand them in, 'just in case they should fall into enemy hands', but I told him I was Royal

Navy and could commandeer them if I wanted to. So, being a loyal subject of King George, he let me have one at 'cost price', making some remark about not wanting the Royal Navy to get lost on the highways and byways of the British Isles, 'Just in case you should happen to run aground'.

When I had got back aboard LB13 I again sat down at the chart table, got out my newly purchased road atlas, and simply looked at the back page on which there was transcribed: 'A Clear and Concise Map of Great Britain', and which showed there was 3 miles to each inch on the map. But with all my years of experience at sea, I knew that the seas around the 7,000-mile coastline of the British Isles are among the most difficult in the world to navigate. Frequent fogs, shallow inshore waters and choppy sea waves create unpredictable hazardous conditions for coasters, barges and even more so for small craft. (Large ocean going vessels would never venture close to the shore down the North Sea coast, outside the buoyed sea lanes.) But I thought this gave me a distinct advantage insofar as I should avoid most types of mines, submarines and E-Boats; but Luftwaffe aircraft I knew couldn't be avoided if they spotted us.

The maximum speed I calculated Tom could get out of LB13 was about 6 knots. I deduced this from the simple fact that the distance between Rosyth and Leith, skirting round the Black Rocks, across the Firth of Forth by boat was between 12 and 15 miles, at a rough guess. It had taken just over two hours, on an ebb tide, to cover that distance. What this meant was that I could make approximately 36 miles running with an ebbing tide, and 36 miles on a rising tide, or something like at least 72 miles if we sailed her for twelve hours a day, at an average speed of 3 knots per twenty-four hours. I looked at the date on a copy of *The Times* newspaper Mattie had left on the chart table. It read Monday 20 May 1940.

The road map I'd purchased indicated the distance from Edinburgh to London was approximately 392 miles by road (628km). So it seemed to me that the coastal sea route down the east coast would be about 404 miles (646km) to Southend-on-Sea in the Thames estuary, from the estuary of the Firth of Forth. Taking my starting point to be near Dunbar, it would be close on 460 miles (736km) from Rosyth to Tilbury. I calculated that, with a bit of luck, it should take between six and seven days' sailing time. I decided to set sail the following morning on top of the flood tide, just as it was about to ebb. In that way I would extract the most benefit from using the ebb tide to take LB13 out into the North Sea, turn to starboard to go south round Fidra lighthouse and North Berwick, a distance I'd calculated to be 18 miles (about 29km), with a further 18 miles taking me down the coast between Bass Rock and Tantallon Castle on towards Reed Point (according to my *Ordnance Survey Road Map of Great Britain*). Then, remembering the charts and compass, I shoved them in a draw under the chart table, and turned in for the night.

I was woken by Mattie at 5a.m. with a mug of tea. Mattie had obviously pre-empted my plan.

'It's a simply lovely day, Skip,' she said. 'Tom's cooking breakfast, the tide is about half an hour off its high water mark, and as soon as we've had our meal, we shall be ready to cast off.'

'What is the date today?' I asked her.

'Tuesday, 21 May 1940,' she replied, 'and the news from France is that our troops are carrying out a strategic withdrawal. It doesn't say where they are withdrawing to, but I think they are heading for the north French coast.'

I got up, had a quick rinse, gobbled my breakfast, washed it down with a mug of hot sweet tea, and ordered Tom to get down to his engine room and start the engine, and for Mattie to cast off. The tide was just on the ebb and I wanted to make North Berwick on the falling tide so I could catch the rising tide as I turned LB13 south down the North Sea coast towards Reed Point.

The going was good as we pulled out of the Firth of Forth, although there was a fresh breeze blowing. The water was a bit choppy as we turned out of the estuary and rounded the point near Dunbar; it was then the fun began as LB13 began to roll about in the cross current. Tom came out of the engine room and made for the lea side of the boat. First he vomited his breakfast over the side, had a couple of minutes rest and then brought up his supper. Then, after a short interlude, his previous day's lunch was ejected. The poor chap, if he had had to vomit again, I'm sure his feet would have been next to get the heave-ho over the side − after which he lay down on the deck exhausted and prayed to God to finish him off.

'I'll make for calmer water inshore, Tom,' I told him; but he either didn't hear me or care. It was obvious too that Tom wasn't a sailor. We'd only travelled about 20 miles in reasonably calm waters and he was really in a bad way. Mattie, who had been busying herself on deck for'ard, came astern and saw Tom lying in the scupper.

'What's wrong with him, Skip?' she asked me. 'Hurt himself, has he?'

'He's been seasick; he thinks he's dying.'

'Oh,' replied Mattie. 'He'll soon get over that. Have you told him Lord Nelson was always seasick when he put to sea?'

'I didn't know he was,' I told her, 'but you can tell him.'

Mattie shrugged her shoulders and smiled, 'I'll tell him a bit later when he feels better,' and she went on with her self-imposed chores of splicing rope ends which she attached to the boats rails, until I ordered her to go down and keep an eye on the diesel engine, which had been working perfectly well without Tom in attendance.

I was quite impressed with Mattie. She knew a lot about boats, although she kept her own wise counsel as to where she had learnt her seamanship. Any fool could have seen she had never been a wage-earning seaman, but with her skill and knowledge of deck work, she could have blended in with any ship's crew, on any ship, anywhere on this earth, had she been a man.

As we slowly edged our way down the North Sea, the weather decided to turn a bit nasty. The wind veered round from north-east to east, and as LB13 was making way with the ebb tide, we began to get heavy spray breaking over the bow and the port side, and the boat began to roll dangerously until I brought her round and sailed her full into the rolling waves, with the east wind blowing into the boat's bow. As I was carrying out this manoeuvre, Mattie came out of the engine room on to the deck and helped Tom to pick himself up from out of the scuppers, taking him below into the cabin and putting him as close to the centre of gravity as she could, so as to reduce the centrifugal force on Tom by the corkscrew movement of the boat. It became obvious to me that if the weather was going to persist in this way we were going to have to work the boat on both states of the tides, the ebb and flow that is, each day, to get her down to Tilbury within the ten-day deadline set by the Admiralty.

The weather held like that until the tide turned, and I was force to turn into it, but once I'd got her round and was running against the tide and the wind, LB13 seemed to leap over the waves, and except for the steeplechase effect as she went over the watery hurdles, and the thump as she landed in the next trough, we rode out the storm without mishap. However, the good news, as far as my crew and I were concerned, was that we were well past Berwick-on-Tweed and had sighted Alnmouth. So I decided to pull into the harbour for a good night's rest, and to give Tom a chance to get over his seasickness; and, for me to have a meal, a meal incidentally that had already been prepared for me by Mattie.

After I'd got the boat tied up by the harbour wall, and once we had eaten our meal, cleared the chart table of platters, condiments and other utensils and washed up, Mattie and I then took a swim in the sea. Tom, on the other hand, had fallen asleep in his bunk, as LB13 rolled gently back and forth against the harbour wall, like a child's cradle in a nursery. 'He'll be as fit as a fiddle in the morning,' Mattie said, and we each turned into our own bunks for the night.

It was as Mattie had predicted. Tom was alive and well next morning, though weak from his efforts to turn himself inside out on the previous day. Mattie had prepared breakfast of eggs, bacon and fried bread, with a mug of tea for herself and me, and a slice of toast for Tom. She told Tom, 'You'd better let your tummy settle down before eating a large meal. We'll be heading out to sea soon, and we don't want a repeat of yesterday's episode of over-reaching ourselves, do we old chap?' Tom nodded in agreement. 'No,' he replied, and went into the engine room to start the diesel motor.

'Where are we headed for today, Skip?' Mattie asked.

'I want to make it to Whitby by nightfall,' I told her. 'We'll go out as soon as the tide's on the ebb, and when it turns on the floe, we'll turn back with it. By the time it reaches high tide again, we should be as near Whitby as damn it.'

'Ah,' said Mattie, 'you're bouncing this old lady along the coast to gain more mileage; actually that's what I would have done had I been in command. Good thinking, Skip.'

It stuck out a mile: Mattie was either a good amateur seaman, or a professional; it was also obvious from her public school background she wasn't an ordinary seaman such as I, who earned his living from the sea, not Mattie. But it was good for me to have her aboard: nothing was too much trouble for her to do and, as things worked out, it was a great stroke of good luck, too.

I followed my sailing plan on our second day, using the tides to leapfrog along the east coast. Tom's 'tummy' had settled down, but Mattie would only allow him light, non-greasy meals, telling him he would, or should be, free of the effects of seasickness by the next day, when he could get back to a normal meal pattern. In this unorthodox way we made Whitby by nightfall, and having tied up for the night, we all went in for a swim, had a light meal and made our way to the nearest pub for a cool, refreshing pint or two of beer, or in Mattie's case a glass of gin and tonic.

My target port for the next day was Grimsby, or to give the town its correct name, Great Grimsby. It was our third day out from Leith and I had to make Grimsby in order to stay within my sailing schedule, but like most things that are planned with scrutiny and care, one can never be sure they will work, especially in wartime.

We were about 3 miles off the shore, just below Scarborough, when we heard an explosion. Mattie and I came out of the cabin and jumped up on top of it. Mattie, as cool as a cucumber, put her hand to her ear then said, 'It sounded like a bomb blast, about 2 miles away. Where are your binoculars, Skip?'

'In the chart table draw,' I said, and jumping down off the cabin roof, I quickly retrieved them, passed them up to Mattie and asked, 'What can you see?'

'It's a collier, on fire and sinking. Change course, Skip. Make for that black smoke on the horizon.' I turned the boat in the direction she was pointing, and within half an hour we were close up to the sinking ship. There were a few blokes in the water amidst a jumble of wreckage. The surface of the water was black with coal dust and oil. The men in the water were buoyed up by their life jackets, while some of the crew who had managed to lower a lifeboat were rowing round in circles among the floating wreckage, trying to pick up some of their shipmates.

'Get the boat hook and pull them in close to the side of the boat. We'll then be able to pull them up out of the sea,' I ordered Mattie. 'We can take the lifeboat in tow as soon as we've got those other chaps out of the water. You'd better hurry, that bloody ship's on the point of sinking.' Then I called down to Tom, 'Idle the engine and come up and give Mattie and me a hand.'

We picked up fifteen seamen out of the water, all that we could find before the ship went down, and there were ten in the lifeboat. Tom went below to get us underway, while Mattie made the lifeboat fast to our stern, then she did what she could to help those men in need of medical treatment. She had obviously had some training in administering first aid, and as she carried out her Florence Nightingale duties, we slowly made our way to the nearest coastal town that was, if I remember rightly, a place called Amble.

'Where's Amble, Jack?' one of the men asked.

It's well up the North Sea coast from the Thames, in Northumberland, not far from Blyth if I remember correctly. It was a bit of a grimy place at the time, with coal exporting quays. However, to continue, I asked the survivors who were sprawled out on the foredeck if the ship's captain was among them. An old man, covered in oil and coal dust, who was obviously in a bad way, answered:

'I'm the captain.'

'I'm sorry, sir. But I've got to write you up in my log,' I told him. 'Who are you, and what are the names of the surviving members of your crew we've picked up, and the name of your ship?' Although he wasn't at all well, still he gave me all the information I required to fill in my log.

At Amble we disgorged the collier's survivors, who were ordered by a police constable to wait to be picked up and driven off in the back of an army lorry. By this time quite a few civilians had gathered on the quayside, and when we pulled alongside some of the local women were soon giving the survivors hot cups or mugs of tea. They had obviously heard the explosion and come to investigate, but they were not surprised to see a boat pull in with survivors from a sunken ship. It was obviously something that was happening on a regular basis now we were at war. What did surprise them, though, was my refusal to come ashore before continuing my journey south. But as I told the police constable, I was under strict orders and had to continue my journey.

Paratrooper Sidney Bardoe, 6th Airborne Division, with WREN Kay Bardoe, 1943. (By kind permission of Sidney and Kay Bardoe)

WREN Kay Bardoe with friends. (By kind permission of Sidney and Kay Bardoe)

'Where are you bound?' he had casually asked.

I smiled and said, 'I could have you locked up for asking me that question, constable, as well you may know. So mind your own bloody business.' I'd always wanted to talk to a copper like that, knowing on this occasion I had more authority than him.

'Oh yes,' he replied, with more of a smirk than a smile. 'Then on your way, sailor.'

Mattie was already at the boat's helm. Tom had pre-empted my order and started the engine. 'I say, constable,' Mattie requested in that Oxford accent of hers, 'would you mind dreadfully letting go the bow and stern lines?' The constable, to my everlasting surprise, gave her a puzzled look; his face broke out in a broad grin and the old sot did as he'd been asked and let go of our mooring lines, gave us a wave of his hand before saying, 'Good luck.'

'Half astern,' I told Mattie, and as LB13 went astern away from the quay, I ordered 'full-a-port', and as we turned half circle, 'starboard half', and we glided away from the small harbour of Amble out into the North Sea. I took the wheel from Mattie and eased LB13 to starboard and headed for Grimsby, keeping the shoreline well within sight. I had never intended to go outside the pre-war coastal navigational channels, and with LB13's shallow draft it was totally unnecessary anyway. Mattie soon got to work, washing away the oil and coal dust off the deck, aided by Tom, and they soon had the deck looking as clean as it had been before our encounter with the coal- and oil-plastered survivors of the ill-fated collier.

After we had proceeded along the coast for a couple of miles, we ran into a blanket of thick sea fog, and I completely lost my bearings. The sea was a bit choppy though, and was showering the foredeck with fine salt spray. After we had been going for about three hours Mattie asked, 'Where are we, Skip?'

'In the North Sea somewhere,' was my reply.

'Lost at sea, are we?' she laughed.

'Well,' I said, 'I can't see the shore.'

'Don't worry about that, Skip. As long as the compass shows we are going south, when we come out of the fog we'll soon get our bearings. It's four hours into the ebb tide now, with two hours to go before the tide begins to flow, and if we follow the pattern you set when we started this journey, we will not be far off of Grimsby by tonight.' Then she added with a laugh, 'Hopefully.' So I sailed on in fearful ignorance of our position or our whereabouts, except for Tom who said:

'I don't care where we are, Skip. I've every confidence in you. You will find our whereabouts when the fog lifts, I've no doubt,' and he went back down into the engine room with a mug of hot tea in one hand and his fingers crossed on the other, to sit and listen to the steady throb of his diesel engine.

The ebbing tide suddenly began to turn, and was now beginning to flow, as we drifted along with it. The fog had started to lift too. It was about three hours on the flood when Mattie said, 'We're off Flamborough.'

'How do you know that?' I asked her.

'Count the flashes from the lighthouse: four quick flashes of about one second each, then a four-second gap, then four more flashes and so on, that's Flamborough Head Lighthouse. Another two hours and we should be in Grimsby.' Then she said, 'That was a nice little surprise for you, wasn't it Skip?' And she laughed. I hadn't seen any flashes from a lighthouse, so I ignored her simply because it was obvious she had known where we were all the time.

We came within sight of Great Grimsby, which is situated on the south side of the River Humber, at about eight o'clock in the evening. We hadn't had time during the day to cook a meal and we were all famished. As we came alongside a fish quay, I told Tom to cut the engine then gave the order, 'Every man for himself to the nearest fish and chip shop,' and we all jumped ashore and ran up the quay steps, me in front, Tom behind and Mattie following. Fortunately I looked round to see how far the other two were behind me, and saw LB13 drifting away from the quay with the falling tide.

'Jesus Christ, Mattie, you've not made her fast,' I called back at her. 'Go back and get her.'

'Oh! Damn it,' I heard her shout, and as she turned back she called out, 'Get me a bag of plaice, chips and a bread roll,' and with those last few words she ran back down the quay, and dived into the River Humber to retrieve our boat. I knew I could rely on her to do what had to be done to get LB13 berthed back alongside the fish quay.

Tom and I soon found a fish and chip shop, put in our orders, gathered up our purchases and made our way back to the boat as quickly as we could. LB13 was tied up to the quay; Mattie had dried herself off after her gallant exploit of retrieving the boat, and she had a big pot of tea ready for us when we got back aboard. We spread our fish and chip supper over the chart table. Mattie poured a mug of tea each for us and we gorged ourselves till we were bloated. We must have looked like a trio of Hermann Goerings sitting there, slowly supping our tea and then dozing away in the oblivion of deep sleep inflicted on us by our own form of internal, contented mesmerism; or perhaps it was due to the ordeal we'd undergone during that day.

None of us woke up until we heard the heavy thumping of sea boots on the deck early the following morning, and the cabin door was slid open.

'What are you doing?' a voice was asking. 'You can't tie up here, this is a fish dock, and trawlers will be coming in on the tide.'

'Well,' I replied, 'first we're here on His Majesty's Service, so we'll do whatever is necessary to fulfil His Majesty's pleasure; second, we can tie up here if it is necessary for us to carry out duties on behalf of His Majesty, and; thirdly, we'll be under way in about an hour, with the turn of the tide – by the way, you haven't got a crate of cod to spare, have you?'

'And a newspaper, please,' Mattie called out.

Like most fishermen he didn't have much to say, and without so much as another word he stepped ashore, went slowly up the quay steps, and came back a few minutes later with a box of mixed fish and a copy of the *Daily Herald*, which he handed to me. I put the fish down on the deck and looked at the newspaper and the date. It read Thursday 23 May 1940. I read the headlines, which showed the news from France wasn't good. Our army was in retreat. I asked the fisherman: 'How much do we owe you?' The fisherman just waved his hand and walked away, but when he got to the top of the quay steps he turned and said, 'Keep an eye open for mines when you get out in the estuary – there were Jerry planes about a couple of nights ago, safe sailing,' and he disappeared out of sight.

We, all three of us, then went out on deck and dived over the side for a quick swim. We had found it was much simpler than trying to wash in the cramped space of the small boat's cabin and less embarrassing for Mattie. When we had got back on board we had a light breakfast of Kellogg's Corn Flakes, egg on toast and a mug of tea each. Then Tom went into the engine room and started the engine; Mattie slipped our moorings; I took the helm and rang the telegraph, and LB13 was under way.

We headed slowly down the dredged channel out of Grimsby, just as the tide began to fall, heading for our next port of call, which was to be Lowestoft. As far as I was concerned, this meant sailing out into the North Sea with the falling tide, then turning in towards Skegness, before crossing the mouth of the Wash and rounding the point at Cromer, before edging along the coast to Lowestoft. However, it wasn't to be plain sailing, not with a bloody war going on. We had got out to sea and were about 2 miles off shore when Mattie called out in that serene voice of hers: 'You had better turn to starboard, and go full astern Skip, there's a mine on the surface about a quarter of a league away.'

'A quarter of a league. Who the bloody hell do you think you are, Jules Verne's Captain Nemo? How far is that mine away, in English please?' I demanded.

'660 fathoms.'

'How far?' I replied, laughing.

'1,320 yards and closing,' she then said. 'Do you want that broken down into feet and inches, Skip?'

'No, don't bother,' I replied. 'I can multiply by three and twelve.'

I turned LB13's wheel hard to starboard and rang the telegraph for Tom to put the engine full astern, and we began to veer away from the mine – or so we thought, but the damn thing began to follow us.

'How much water have we got under us, Mattie?' I asked.

Mattie threw a depth gauge over the side. 'It's varying between 1½ and 2 fathoms, Skip. I think that mine's lost its anchor cable, and we're running over a sand bank, but the tide's on the make so if we can run before it at a steady 6 knots, we should be able to keep a cable's distance away from it.'

'A cable's distance, Skip?' Mattie asked. 'What's that in English?'

'About 100 fathoms,' I replied.

'Can I have that in yards, Skip?'

I realised she was extracting the proverbial urine and told her: 'Don't you come the old madam with me, sailor – even public schoolgirls are taught to multiply by two. Now don't you be cheeky or I'll put you on a charge for insubordination.'

'You won't need to if that mine catches us up,' Mattie laughed. 'I think it's gaining on us, but it shouldn't come near us – LB13's a clinker-built wooden boat with not much metal in her, at least not enough to attract a magnetic mine.'

'Oh my God,' I exclaimed. 'So what about those steel plates we put aboard as ballast?'

'Yes, of course. I'd forgotten about them,' she said. 'I'll get down below and pass some of them up. We'd better throw them overboard.'

'A good idea,' I said. We had ejected two or three pieces of the steel plates into the sea when Tom stuck his head out of the engine room hatch.

'What on earth are you doing, Skip?' he asked.

'Jettisoning some of this steel plate – that mine we saw is following us; it must be a magnetic mine.'

Tom burst out laughing, 'I might not know a lot about boat engines,' he said, 'but I do know about mines – especially magnetic mines. I did a short course in mine disposal in Portsmouth

Naval Barracks. The magnetic mine, for instance, is a form of non-contact mine. It's usually laid on the seabed. It contains a delicate magnetic needle, sufficiently sensitive to respond to a change in a magnetic field when a ferrous object passes over it. This change causes an electrical contact to close, and that's what detonates the explosive charge in the mine. I wouldn't throw anything else over the side, Skip. That mine shouldn't bother us.'

I shrugged my shoulders and said, 'Okay. I'll take your word for it, Tom.' I had just turned my back on the mine when there was a hell of an almighty bang astern. The mine had exploded; it not only caused a water spout that went at least 100ft into the air, but it also caused a tidal wave that washed over LB13's stern and sent her skipping over the water at about 12 knots.

Mattie, in her calm, serene voice, said, 'After another two or three explosions like that, Skip, we could be going up the Thames in the morning. Not much to be said for short courses in mine disposal, is there? That steel plate we threw overboard must have triggered it off, do you think?'

'Possibly, Mattie,' I said, and thought I had left it at that for the moment, but Tom popped his head out of the engine room to ask: 'Why are we bobbing about like a cork?' And, 'did I hear an explosion?'

'Yes you did, Tom,' I told him, 'And that brings me to a reluctant conclusion.'

'What's that?' he asked, in all innocence.

'Not only don't you know much about boat engines, but I'm of the opinion that you're not too well informed with regard to your knowledge of the mechanics relating to *magnetic mines*.'

But before he could reply Mattie called out sharply: 'Grab one of those rope lines and get over the side; there's a German aircraft diving down at us, an ME 109, quickly.'

We each grabbed a rope line and dived over the side just as the ME 109 let rip at us with its machine guns. Thankfully most of the bullets missed LB13, making small splashes in the water all round us as they gave off a series of loud plops. We waited in the water for a few minutes, until we heard the aircraft's engines fade in the distance. We then scrambled back aboard the boat.

Mattie laughed and casually said, 'That was rather close, wasn't it Skip? I do suppose that German pilot saw the waterspout when that mine exploded and came to investigate.'

'Yes, Mattie,' I replied, 'and I was wondering earlier on why you were making those ropes up and securing them along the boat's rails, now I know. That's what I call pre-empting an event.' And those were the last words we spoke to each other until we were pulling into Lowestoft on our fourth day at sea, Friday 24 May 1940.

'Why did you put into Lowestoft, Jack?' he was asked. 'Why not Great Yarmouth? It's a bigger port than Lowestoft.'

'Because,' replied Jack, 'I didn't want to get stuck on any of the sandbanks outside the harbour, or in the approach channel. Mattie had warned me about them, she had said if we got beached on a shingle bank as the tide fell, we would have to spend at least six hours marooned out there – that's why I chose to pull into Lowestoft. Lowestoft is, after all, only 9 miles from Great Yarmouth.'

'Was that the only reason, Jack?' another of his enthralled audience asked.

'Well,' he said. 'To be truthful, no. Mattie had told me she knew of a nice, snug hostelry where we could get a decent meal, a pint of beer, have a real bath and get a bed for the night. I

WREN Kay Bardoe
and friend, 1940. (By
kind permission of
Sidney and Kay Bardoe)

told her I couldn't afford such luxuries, but she insisted, saying: "I know the owner quite well,
Skip. I'm sure he'll accommodate us for a night." So, when we had pulled in alongside a quay
and made the boat secure, we followed Mattie into the town.'

The hostelry she took us to was on the north side of a bridge, close to the small harbour
and a railway station. It turned out to be the Suffolk Hotel, a really posh place by anybody's
standard, where Mine Host greeted Mattie with a warm smile and kissed her hand. Tom and I
were told to bring in madam's portmanteau, but Mattie quickly put things right by explaining
that we were her shipmates, that I was the Skipper of the boat and Tom the engineer, and that
we wanted rooms for the night, with a bath. That immediately changed everything and we
were shown into a side room, where in large gold letters painted on the door were the words:
'Private – Director's Office.'

Once inside Mine Host's office, he explained that the hotel had been set aside for officers only. So if madam wouldn't mind being patient, things would be arranged to madam's satisfaction. Mattie laughed and said she understood, but could we have two pints of his best beer and half a pint to start with, and the menu. 'Beer?' Mine Host had asked in surprise. 'Surely two pints of beer and your usual tipple, madam?'

'No, Charles,' Mattie had said, 'two pints and one half of beer.'

'Yes, madam,' Charles had replied, and hurried off without further ado to surreptitiously arrange things.

Within a few minutes a pretty waitress appeared. She had two pints of beer on a silver tray, a half pint in a cut glass tumbler and three menus, all written in French. She curtsied to Mattie whom she obviously knew, and smiled at Tom and me as we sat staring at the menus. Mattie looked at each of us in turn, smiled and said, 'Shall I order, Skip?'

'I think you better had,' I agreed, and Mattie ordered soup and lightly grilled sirloin steak with all the trimmings for all three of us. She told the waitress, 'Ask the chef to prepare our meal as quickly as he can, and we'll have two bottles of claret, too, if we may.'

The waitress, with a 'Yes, madam', left the room with a broad smile on her face, just as Mine Host returned. He informed Mattie that he had arranged our accommodation, and after we had eaten a sumptuous meal, washed down with wine, that was followed by gateau with cream, cheese and biscuits with coffee and Drambuie liqueur, we were shown to our bedrooms (via a back staircase) by elderly porters (all of whom looked as if they had been brought out of Egyptian mummy caskets), where pyjamas had been laid out on the beds. After telling a porter I wished to be called at five o'clock the next morning, I had my first real bath for a week, dried myself off, crawled into bed and slept the sleep of death until I was awakened at five the next morning by the bed-side telephone. 'Good morning, sir,' a woman's voice said. 'This is your 5a.m. call.'

When I got down to the breakfast room, Mattie and Tom were already seated, stuffing themselves with porridge, eggs and bacon, followed by marmalade on toast.

Apparently Mine Host had asked Mattie if we could leave the hotel before the officers came down to 'breakers', because if we were caught in the hotel we would all be for the high jump, him and us. So we finished our meal, thanked and said goodbye to Mine Host, who gave a slight bow to Mattie with a 'Good to see you again, madam', before he disappeared back into the hotel foyer.

'That's a nice place, Mattie,' I said, 'but don't they know there's a war on in Lowestoft, and that the rest of the country are on rations? And don't we have to pay for our stay and our meals?'

'The answers to your questions are: "Not for officers of his majesty's armed forces, Skip" and: "I know the owner of the hotel, he'll settle the bill for us".'

However, as we walked from the hotel towards the quay, where LB13 was berthed, we were literally pounced on by 'crushers' (naval Military Police).

'Now where do you two jolly jack tars think you're off to, with this wren?' the jaunty in charge of the patrol demanded to know.

'To that boat tied up to the quay,' I told him. But he was very suspicious.

'Where are your papers?' And 'Who's in command of the boat?'

I gave him my papers, which he scrutinised, then the letter which contained my orders. He looked me up and down in my seaman's uniform, before handing my documents back to me, with a quizzical look on his face. He then checked first Tom's papers, then Mattie's. He stared at Mattie in her seaman's uniform and said, 'Thank you, madam. That will be all. You may go.' With those last few kind words we quickly marched off along the quay, scrambled down the quay steps and, watched by the crushers, we stepped aboard LB13 to prepare her for the next stage of our epic journey. Then Mattie said:

'I think someone must have informed the naval authorities we were at the hotel last night. After all, it's not often one has the privilege of being molested by a ship's master at arms at six o'clock in the morning, is it?' The date was Saturday 25 May 1940.

I decided that I should avoid putting in to any more North Sea ports or seaside resorts, and sailed on past Southwold, Thorpe Ness and Aldeburgh, before cutting across the coastal sand spit of Orford Ness off the Suffolk coast. I followed the London sailing barges' route back down the final stretch of the east coast, past the estuary of the River Stour, Walton-on-the-Naze, Clacton-on-Sea and Havengore Creek, which is the seaward limit of the Port of London Authority.

I was in my home territory now. I sailed LB13 on over the Maplin Sands, close to Black Grounds and Pigs Bay. I went round Shoebury Ness, keeping inside the Knock. For now I was without a care in the world. I had entered the Thames estuary, and it wasn't long before Mattie tied LB13 up to Southend pier head, just as the tide was on the last of its ebb.

As soon as the boat had been made secure, I informed my crew: 'I've got to go and make a phone call. You two had better wait here until I come back. I'm reporting in for orders.'

I jumped off LB13's deck on to the lower landing stage of the pier, and ran up to the top deck to make my telephone call. The pier had been closed for the duration of the war to the general public, but the navy had taken it over. I made my way to the pier's restaurant that was being used as an office, and got permission from the officer in charge to make a telephone call through to Chatham Naval Barracks. I was ordered to stay where I was overnight by the duty officer at Chatham, and to make my way to Tilbury Passenger Landing Stage on the following morning tide. I was also informed a naval detachment would be there to receive me. I asked whoever it was on the other end of the line if he would confirm this order with the officer in charge of Southend Pier, which he did. I was given permission to tie up for the night, but that I must sail for Tilbury Passenger Landing Stage on the morning tide (military services always duplicate or triplicate everything).

When I arrived back on board LB13 I told Mattie and Tom what my orders were, and that they must telephone the naval barracks from whence they'd come for orders when we reach Tilbury Passenger Landing Stage. They then went through the formal rigmarole of asking my permission if they could leave the craft to make a telephone call to their base, and of course, now they both knew what my orders were for the following day, there was every need for them to do so.

'Go on then,' I told them. 'That's if that officer in charge up there will let you make a call. She was a bit offish with me. Wanted to know why I was in charge of LB13 (a common ordinary seaman) until I showed her my "letter of authority". That shut her up.' Then I told them, 'Go on. Get it over with.'

With that they went out of the cabin, jumped ashore, skipped up on to the top landing stage level, Mattie one step, Tom two steps at a time. They were gone about an hour before they returned. When they finally staggered back aboard LB13 they were pie-eyed. I was damn annoyed and asked them: 'Where have you two been? It doesn't take this long to make a telephone call.'

'Mattie knew that officer who's in charge of the pier,' Tom slurred. 'They were at the same public school. We had a couple of drinks with her (common seamen that we are). She wanted to know what we had been up to, and why you, a common rating like what you are, is in command of LB13. But Mattie told her it was a "top-secret" operation, and we couldn't divulge anything to anyone, not even her. But Mattie promised her that if they both survived the war, she would tell her what we had been up to when it was all over – so she gave us a few more drinks to loosen our tongues, or so she thought. We left her in her office chair, intoxicated out of her mind. I wouldn't like to have her head when she wakes up in the morning.'

'No,' I told them, 'nor would I like to have yours. Now go to your bunks and try to sleep it off.'

The following morning I had to pull them out of their bunks. They were both moaning and groaning, complaining about their heads. But I told them to pull themselves together or I'd put them on a charge for making themselves unfit for duty aboard HM LB13. I had to get my own breakfast while they sat on deck, drinking black coffee, trying to clear their thick heads. However I was used to drunkenness among seamen. I knew that as soon as we got under way, and they were getting a rush of fresh sea air into their lungs, they would soon sober up.

I had timed my breakfast to coincide with the rise of the tide, so that the water in the estuary, coming in from the North Sea, had time to rise above the level of the water running out of the Thames, creating a 'mini-bore'. That simple technique added momentum to the rising tide and gave extra thrust to the power of LB13's diesel engine, and added a couple of knots to her speed.

As soon as I had finished my breakfast, I gave the order for Tom to start the engine and ordered Mattie to cast off the fore and aft lines that tethered the boat to the pier. I set LB13 on a course along the Essex side of the river, in a thick sea haze that covered the whole of the estuary. It's about 24 miles (38km) from Southend Pier to Tilbury Riverside Passenger Jetty along the north side of the Thames. It's a journey that should take about three hours running with the tide. As we chugged our way slowly up the Thames towards Tilbury, leaving Southend Pier further and further behind us, I moved LB13 over closer to the Essex coast line of the river, keeping inside the buoyed areas well away from the main shipping lane and dredged channel. This was for two reasons: I had no intention of getting my boat run down by a rogue ship running upriver with the tide, or of repeating my experience with the magnetic mine off Grimsby. There were already enough wrecks in the Thames estuary that had been sunk by magnetic mines. I had no intention of adding another one to them.

I kept the old girl hugging the Essex shore, keeping her as close as I dared inside the Chapman Buoy, but well clear of the Chapman Sands. In this way LB13 chugged her way merrily upriver with the tide, past Hole Haven, Horseshoe and the Shell Haven oil refinery, until I turned her round the river's bend off Mucking Creek. I then sailed her across the

Mucking Flats, but kept close to the main dredged shipping lane in Lower Hope Reach; then I sailed her between the Ovens Buoy and the Essex shore, where I rounded the river between East Tilbury Fort, on the Essex shore, and Cliffe and Shorne Mead Forts in Kent, but steering a course that kept LB13 away from the barrier of groynes set in the river off the East Tilbury foreshore.

Finally, when we were on the home stretch, Mattie came into the wheelhouse. She sat down at the chart table next to me, and placing her hand on my arm she said, 'Thank you Jack. It must have been very frustrating for you having me on board.' Then she smiled and sat watching with interest as we sailed past the Ship & Lobster public house on the Kent side of the river, then The World's End public house on the Essex shore close to Tilbury Fort; then passing Gravesend town where I brought LB13 into Gravesend Reach, to turned her round outside the old Tilbury Docks lock entrance into the incoming tide, that was running at about 6 knots. It was a manoeuvre that almost brought LB13 to an abrupt standstill.

Having turned her head into the tide, I brought her back downriver to bring LB13 alongside Tilbury Riverside Landing Stage's western end, keeping her well away from the Tilbury to Gravesend Ferry Terminal. As soon as we came alongside the jetty, Mattie left the wheelhouse and threw the securing lines up on to the landing stage, where two matelots were waiting to make LB13 fast to the landing stage bollards. I was home. The date was Sunday 26 May 1940.

When we arrived there was a Royal Naval contingent on the landing stage to meet us, with a lorry full of stores. There was also a Rolls-Royce motorcar close by, with a naval officer standing by its rear door, and a chauffeur in attendance. The naval contingent was in the

The Ship & Lobster public house. (Author's collection)

charge of a lieutenant, who immediately ordered the three of us ashore together with our kit, and told his matelots to re-fuel and re-store the boat, 'on the double'. Then he told my crew and me he understood we had our orders to return to our own naval barracks, and we must get on our way immediately, because we were on a high alert.

I turned to face my shipmates. Tom and I shook hands. Tom said, 'That's an experience I won't ever forget.'

Mattie said: 'It was good to meet you Mr Hicks', and winked. (She said Mr Hicks not in a nasty way, more in an authoritative way, as if she was used to giving orders.) 'I doubt we shall ever meet again in similar circumstances, but I must say I rather enjoyed the trip.' Then she kissed me on the cheek, smiled and walked off to the Rolls-Royce.

Tom was stunned. He picked up his kit and made his way up the passenger causeway that led to Tilbury Riverside Railway Station, from where he'd catch a train back to Portsmouth via London. He'd walked off without so much as another word. He never even looked back or waved. It was then that the chauffeur of the Rolls-Royce walked over and picked up Mattie's kit, which he carried over to the boot of the car. Mattie followed him to the Rolls-Royce; the chauffeur opened the door for her and Mattie got in. She sat down, lowered the car window and said: 'You're off to Chatham, aren't you, Skip? Otherwise I would have given you a lift.'

'Yes,' I replied, 'where are you bound?'

She smiled. 'Rosyth,' she said, and closed the car window.

I said to the chauffeur in a joking manner, as the limousine was pulling away, 'Mattie is quite a sailor, isn't she?'

That saucy sot looked down his nose at me with a surprised look on his face, and in a supercilious voice said, 'So I understand her ladyship is, sir.' Then he sped away up the landing stage vehicle ramp – and she was gone.

'Oh – goud – blimy Jack. What did you do then?' one of the listeners said.

Jack shrugged his shoulders and replied, 'I turned round and asked the lieutenant: "Where are you bound for in LB13, sir?"'

'For your information, Hicks, and your ears alone. We are to be picked up by a Thames tugboat by the name of *Java*, and towed to a destination on the French coast named Dunkirk.'

'Dunkirk,' I said, 'that's all shallow water and sand along that coastline.'

'Yes,' he replied, 'so I understand. That's why we need small boats with shallow drafts.'

'Then good luck, sir,' I said and walked off along the landing stage to its eastern end, to catch the steam ferry to Gravesend, from where I knew I could get a number 26 Maidstone and District omnibus, to take me back to Chatham Naval Barracks, where I'd revert back to being a common ordinary seaman. But that expedition, I would argue, brothers, was worthy of being considered in the same light as having 'The Nelson Touch': I rest my case.

I looked at my watch; it read a quarter past one o'clock.

'Christ,' I cried out, 'look at the time.' I dashed out of the Port Authority's gear shed on to the quay; fortunately it was snowing, and obviously had been for quite some time, as there were several inches of the white fluffy stuff covering the whole dock area, including the Clan-Line ship. I ran along the quay, climbed the three sections of steel ladders up into the Stothert & Pitt crane cabin, swung the 80ft jib out over the ship's hold to an angry cry from the 'tween

Stowing bag work into Thames lighter, Royal docks, 1940s. (Author's collection)

deck far below of: 'Where the bloody hell have you been? Get the beams and hatches on.' So, as hastily as possible, I did.

In Conclusion

It is a fact that one of the greatest maritime disasters ever recorded was the loss of Convoy PQ17 in July 1942, when twenty-six merchant ships out of thirty-two, together with their crews and cargoes, were lost to enemy action. The blame for this monumental catastrophe has been attributed to a decision made by the First Sea Lord, Sir Dudley Pound, who ordered the Royal Navy's cruiser escort to withdraw from protecting Convoy PQ17, and that the merchant ships of the convoy should scatter.

It is true, too, that Jack (an ordinary seaman in the Royal Navy at the time of this story) was ordered to bring a battered old lifeboat from Scotland, down the east coast of the North Sea and up the Thames to Tilbury Landing Stage.

It is also true the ST *Java*, owned by William Watkins Overseas Towage Ltd, a Gravesend-based ship towage company, was the first of the small ships to reach the Dunkirk beaches. The ST *Java* was just one of the forty-one Thames tugs that took part in the Dunkirk evacuation. She took with her a flotilla of even smaller boats that were used to ferry British, French and Belgian troops off the Dunkirk beaches to be embarked on to larger ships waiting in deeper water, a means by which over 350,000 soldiers were taken off that shallow water and sand-covered French shore.

The Dunkirk evacuation of Allied troops under the code name Dynamo was organised under the direction of Admiral Ramsey at his headquarters within the White Cliffs of Dover. It was an operation that can be described as one of the great naval victories of the Second World War, attributable in full measure to the sailors of the Royal Navy, the tug-boat and life-boat services, mercantile marines and the volunteer owners and crews of the little ships that crossed the 30+ miles of English Channel, risking their all, to bring soldiers of the British and Allied armies back to Britain.

Finally, it is interesting to note that the Women's Royal Naval Service (WRENS) were demobilised after the First World War, but were reformed in April 1939. The main objective of this policy was to release men for active service. The first WRENS were recruited from naval families and attached to most naval shore establishments; others were employed in secret naval intelligence and communication duties, and when necessary as volunteers in ancillary naval attachment duties. No doubt LB13 was one such operation.

TALE 3

BERT'S LAST WAGER

'Is it still damn raining, Bert?' the question came from George, the ship's down-hold foreman, who was sitting on a tea chest in a transit shed, and was addressed to Bert, one of the barge-hands to George's ship's discharging gang.

Bert was standing inside a transit shed doorway, leaning against one of its steel support stanchions, holding his docker's hook in his left hand, while swearing and cursing the weather, as he watched the rain sweep in a continuous sheet across the quayside, bouncing off the deck and the hatch covers of the SS *Ebo*, a ship owned by the Elder Dumpster Shipping Line.

The SS *Ebo* was a passenger/cargo liner that traded between the Port of London's Tilbury Docks and pre-selected ports down the West African coast from Dakar in Senegal, to Luanda in Angola. The ship was secured fore and aft to her discharging berth in Tilbury Docks by wire hawsers and nylon ropes, attached to cast-iron bollards concreted into the quay. From her cargo holds only an hour before, the ship's down-hold gangs had begun to discharge its freight of cocoa beans into Thames lighters, for that expensive commercial commodity's final leg of its sea voyage, upriver, to the import merchants' processing factories.

The freight of cocoa beans had been imported from West Africa, and on being discharged from the SS *Ebo* they were to be transported by Thames lighters to a destination in east London, where they would undergo the process of fermentation, followed by roasting, after which they would be ground down into a fine powder and used in making chocolate, and other food and drink manufactured products. It was an important feature of the discharging operation that the cocoa beans should not become wet or damp, simply because the beans quickly begin to deteriorate, hence the abrupt halt in the cocoa bean discharging operation – a stoppage of work entirely due to the rain storm, which was building up a bout of mental and physical aggression in Bert. Further, the 'over-side' discharging piecework rate paid to dockers for carrying out this particular work operation was 3*s* 1*d* per ton per ship's gang.

'Yer, it's still damn raining,' Bert replied, 'and it won't bloody stop this morning by the looks of it, damn it.' He walked into the transit shed, keeping himself distanced from the other gang members.

Bert wasn't a man to waste words, and generally what he had already said was more than his speech quota for a whole day. He was an odd sort of character, with a curious anti-social disposition, who just didn't appear to like or trust other people – he was a human maverick who always kept his fellow dockers at a distance, never making friends among his contemporaries.

Bert was a loner with a grudge, and it was obvious he could be a very dangerous man if he was antagonised.

To describe a man such as Bert is difficult: he was sort of short to medium in height, that is he was about 5ft 7in (170cm). He weighed something like 14 stone (96.5kg). He had deep brownish-coloured eyes and a pug nose spread evenly across his face, which showed it had received a thump or two in boxing rings or street brawls.

Sadly for Bert, all his facial features appeared to have been etched on to a large swede. It was a concoction of human anatomy, capped with a mop of black wavy hair that was going grey around his ears and neck; a feature, oddly enough, that enhanced the magnificence of his ugliness. One wag had suggested he could have made more money being exhibited in a Chamber of Horror than he could ever get working as a wage slave in the docking industry.

Finally, apart from his unfortunate cosmetic appearance, there were his physical deformities. These included rounded shoulders that caused his head to hang over his chest, reminiscent of Neolithic man. He had long arms that bulged with muscles, and which, from a rear view, gave him the same resemblance to that of a gorilla; on the end of the arms were a pair of hands that, if they had been yellow, anyone would have been forgiven for thinking he was carrying two bunches of bananas.

From his appearance, Bert looked to be what he was: a tough vindictive character with a grudge against society as a whole, and no individual in particular. He was a man who was always on the lookout for a fellow protagonist with whom or on whom he could let vent his intense built-up aggression. That, I must advise the reader, was an ongoing problem in the docking industry. For it was a workplace where virtually every man employed within its walled precincts had been trained during his military service days as an armed assassin, taught by professional instructors employed for that purpose within His Majesty's armed services, on how to kill or to be killed.

'The ship's mate isn't likely to let us open the ship up again in this weather,' George said. 'What about some of us playing a hand or two of cards? It will help to pass the time away till the rain stops.'

This brought a mutter of approval from several members of the ship's gang, who came forward and volunteered to play – seven in fact, which almost made up two sets of players, but they were still one man short.

'We need one more man for a game of cards,' George called out, but nobody else came forward to play.

'What about you, Terry?' said George.

Terry, who was said to be the resident Communist Party member of our ship's gang, with degrees in political economy and philosophy, looked up from scrutinising the contents of his *Daily Worker* newspaper, sneered down his nose, gave George a look of utter contempt, and carried on reading his political bible.

George shrugged his shoulders then said, 'What about you, Bert? A game of cards to pass the time away?'

'No! Not me,' Bert growled, slowly shaking his swede-shaped cranium.

'Why not?' George taunted him. 'I've come to believe there's something very odd about you. You're always looking for trouble, you're as tight as a duck's arse when it comes to parting with your money, and come to think about it I've never seen you have a bet on the dogs or on the horses. In point of fact, I've never seen you have a bet at all, not even in Smoky Joe's café. You won't even play a hand of cards – are you afraid of losing your money?'

Bert walked over to the card school and, raising his big fist, firmly jabbed a banana-sized index finger into George's chest and said: 'Nothing you could do would frighten me.'

George, who had been sitting down, suddenly stood up. He was several inches taller than Bert, and as powerfully built, physically. During his army days he'd been a sergeant major unarmed combat drill instructor. Now he glared down at the smaller man.

'If that's the case, get your money out and play, you tight-fisted little sot,' his attitude was nothing but threatening.

Bert's eyes narrowed, then he said: 'I used to be an idiot like you lot. If anything I was more addicted to gambling than all you put together – I used to take wagers on anything.'

'So what brought about your cure from that addiction?' George said and laughed. 'A trip to Lourdes, was it? Or perhaps it was a long psychiatric session with Sigmund Freud on *The Way We See Ourselves*? Or was it because you woke up one night from dreaming you were in heaven and thought that you'd "seen the light"? Or is it simply because you really are a tight-fisted, miserly little sot?'

Blood was about to be spilled when one of the other gang members quickly broke into the verbal confrontation with, 'So what cured you of the gambling habit, Bert?'

Bert sat down on a tea chest and began to tell us this story. It was as though he had been waiting for years to unload his burden on to someone, because the words of his tale came out of his mouth so naturally. He began:

It's funny how some people meet, isn't it? I mean, meeting different people appears to be coincidental to most of us, but I'm sure that in most instances it's fate that brings us together for specific purposes. Now take my case as an example. I first met my mate, John Broomfield, at Colchester army barracks in March 1940. We had both recently volunteered for army service. John was an East End Londoner, and I was from Dagenham, Essex. I knew his manor around Stepney pretty well because I was a van boy and worked for the Co-operative Wholesale Society. Our department made deliveries in east London, but John, except for his family's "op pickin' 'olidays" down in Kent, had never been farther than Woolwich before he'd joined up for military service, and that was only because he and his mates used to cross the river on the Woolwich free ferry when they were kids.

We hit it off right away, John and me. In fact I doubt if two young men had ever been more alike in their outlook, without being identical twins that is. We thought alike, we liked the same sort of things, we even looked alike, and we both had a mania for gambling.

'You poor sots,' George said, sympathetically.

Bert ignored him and went on: 'The other lads in our training squad used to rib us about it. They reckoned one of our dads had had a roving eye, and to have looked at us I'm sure they must have been right.'

'Bloody hell,' George blurted out. 'There can't be another freak walking about looking like you, can there?'

Bert either didn't hear the outburst or ignored it and continued, 'But the one thing we were both mostly attracted to was gambling, and it was the gambling bug that parted us in the end.'

'How did that come about?' one other member of the gang asked.

Well, after we had been at the army training camp for a few weeks, we had become recognised as the unit bookmakers. We would take bets on anything or anyone: for example, who would be first to be absent without leave, who'd be in the first on an overseas draft, you know the sort of thing. I mean, once we even took bets with a whole platoon that we could get our sergeant to miss what they all thought was his favourite sport – turning over our newly laid out clean and blancoed kit when he did his daily inspection.

Our sergeant training instructor was an old regular, and had served in the army since the First World War. That, as it turned out, was to our advantage, because it allowed us to lengthen the betting odds in our favour. What we had to do first was to find the sergeant's weak points in order to achieve our purpose. John and I, when we were cleaning our kit, racked our brains for the solution to the problem. Then he suddenly hit on a brilliant idea:

'I've got it, Bert,' he said. 'You leave it to me, mate; just leave it to me.' He got up and, hee-hawing like a donkey with a bunch of fresh carrots, he virtually threw himself out of our marquee, as though all the dogs of hell were at his heels.

On the following day the kit inspection was carried out as per usual, but by a second lieutenant and a corporal – our illustrious sergeant was noticeable by his absence. I couldn't think how our luck had been so quick in coming, because when John had arrived back in the marquee, he hadn't said anything more to me about the affair, he had happily collected our winnings during 'Blanco time' in the big tent that was our temporary home until we had finished our basic training.

It was then when we were sitting on our bunks, cleaning our brasses and blancoing our webbings the following evening, that the sergeant appeared at the entrance to our marquee.

''Ten-shun,' the sergeant's voice bellowed out.

We shot up from our bunks on to our feet and stood like ramrods waiting for his next kind words.

'Right,' he roared. 'Which one of you clever young bastards sent me a telegram saying my wife had just given birth to twins?'

Not one word was uttered by any of the men in the marquee, but their eyes all slowly worked their way towards the corner of their sockets, which was in mine and John's direction; the sergeant's head and eyes followed them.

'Oh. So it was you young pair of bastards, was it? Get over to my office on the double. Now,' he shouted at the top of his voice. John and I went out through the marquee flap with the speed of light infantrymen, and with the sergeant bellowing behind us 'left right, left right, left right', until we got up to his office door then 'halt' and we stood marching on the spot until he opened the hut door and barked the order, 'get inside'.

We marched into his office and stood to attention in front of his desk; he followed us in and walked round us, sizing us up before he sat down. His eyes didn't leave us for a second.

'Right now! What's your flaming game?' he demanded to know. I left it to John to explain. After John had told him about the bets we had taken on with the platoon and the need for 'his good self' to be absent from the kit inspection, the sergeant's face broke into a crafty smile and he winked at us. 'Oh!' he said. 'That's all it was then, a bit of a caper – eh, a boyish prank, no harm meant and no damage done.'

'That's right, sergeant,' said John. 'No 'arm meant. It was just for a bet.'

'Oh I see. Just for a jolly old wager, was it? By the way, how much did you make at my expense?' the sergeant demanded to know, his eyes narrowing into what was a positive threat.

'Twenty quid, sergeant,' John replied.

'Mm, now,' he said. 'I'm a gambling man myself and like to have a wager occasionally, so this is what I'll do. I bet you two twenty quid that if I report this prank of yours to the CO, you will both get six months in a "glass house". You may think I'm a hard disciplinarian, but you wait till those Redcaps get hold of you in a Military Prison, then you'll think I've been giving you the kid-glove treatment.'

John, as quick as a flash, put his hand into his tunic pocket and brought out four of the old white £5 notes. 'No need for that sergeant; we accept that bet,' he replied and placed the money on his desk.

'It's a wager then,' the sergeant said, and picked up the cash.

'Yes, you're on, sergeant,' John replied, and made to shake hands on the deal. The sergeant ignored him.

'Get out of here, and don't you ever try any of those tricks on me again, or I'll have the pair of you roasted alive, get me?' He was roaring at us as though he was a mad bull.

We didn't wait for a second longer, just in case he changed his mind. We went out of his office faster than a pair of greyhounds rounding the bend at a White City race meeting. When we had got back in the marquee, we dropped down on our bunks gasping for breath and wheezing like a pair of old steam engines. When I'd got my breath back, I said to John, 'I thought we'd made thirty quid on those bets?'

'Yes Bert, we did. But the sergeant wasn't to know that, was he? He may have got twenty quid, but at least we got a fiver each.' And putting his hand once again into his tunic pocket, he passed me a nice, crisp, white £5 note.

'Well, at least we managed to salvage something out of those bets we took on, John,' I told him. 'By the way, I thought the sergeant was a bit upset about those twins you foisted on to him, didn't you?'

'So would you have been if you was him,' John winked. 'You see, when I left you the day before yesterday, I made a few enquiries about our sergeant. I discovered his wife was living in army married quarters in Woolwich Barracks, in Kent. What's more, the sergeant had been abroad in India for twelve months and had only had his first leave six months ago. I telephoned one of my mates in the East End, he works on the south side of the Thames just outside Blackball Tunnel, and he sent a telegram for me to the sergeant here at Colchester Barracks, telling him his wife had had twins. The sergeant was given instant compassionate leave, and shot off home as fast as a bullet from a rifle, no doubt with murder on his mind. That's what got him away from the kit inspection.' John looked through the marquee flap entrance, back towards the sergeant's office, and then added, 'I always thought that sergeant was a real vicious, vindictive, callous old bastard, but he had us bang to rights just now, and he let us off. I won't forget that in a hurry.'

'It cost us twenty quid just the same,' I pointed out.

John winked and said, 'We'll have to put that down to wetting the babies' heads, won't we?'

He was a fine fellow and a loyal mate, was John.

'He *was* a fine fellow?' George ventured to ask.

'Yes, he *was* a fine fellow,' Bert replied, his mind recollecting memories of his wartime experiences. 'After completing our initial training,' he continued, 'we were sent to Salisbury Plain for tactical training before being given the obligatory twenty-one days embarkation leave; then we were shipped out to Egypt via the long sea route, which meant sailing down the west coast of Africa, round the Cape of Good Hope, and up the African east coast into the Red Sea. Our destination was initially Egypt, and we arrived there in August 1940. It was a good trip, with only a few scares when U-boats were reported to be about, but John and I, we ran a betting book on the trip, and that took our minds off that sort of thing.'

When we arrived in Egypt, we found General Sir Archibald Wavell was in overall command of what was then known as the Imperial Army. The Imperial Army was made up of British, Australian, New Zealand and Indian troops, and the British 7th Armoured Division equipped with Matilda tanks, which were under the command of General Creagh, and the 11th Hussars Armoured Car Regiment, under the command of Lieutenant Colonel Combe.

However, the overall commander of the Imperial Army was General O'Connor, whose leadership was responsible for our victories once the real fighting started against the Italians. We troops of the Imperial Army had a fine old time, chasing the Italians from one of their fortifications to another. We British troops captured Birdie, in January 1941; Tobruk was taken by the Australians, also in January 1941. The Australians were under the command of a General MacKay and had the armoured support of the 7th Royal Tank Regiment, which led the attack with their Matilda tanks. Benghazi was taken in February and these victories virtually brought about the final destruction of Italian forces in Cyrenaica. So you see, we young blokes were soon blooded in a few weeks of hectic fighting and were beginning to settle down like real veterans. Now I come to think of it, most of them were, because almost all of them had served in France and Belgium, and at least two of them were in Second Lieutenant Duckier Annand's platoon, on the south side of the River Dyle in May 1940 when he won a Victoria Cross using hand grenades to stop German engineers repairing the bridge that crossed the river. Some of our platoon had been among the British Expeditionary Force (BEF) evacuated off the Dunkirk beaches in May and June 1940. That March 1941 was a time the Imperial Army spent clearing up the aftermath of the battles: burying the dead and sorting out the prisoners. But battles continued to be fought as the Italians fell back into Ethiopia. On 1 April our armies occupied Asmara before they pushed on eastward to capture Massawa. The Italian army surrendered on 8 April 1941 and that ended the Eritrea campaign. But in March 1941 the Germans had landed in Libya with their Panzers under the command of General Erwin Rommel, later to become known among British troops as the Desert Fox.

The Germans were a different kettle of fish to the Italians altogether, and our battalion was rushed from Asmara in Eritrea to Libya, just in time to meet the German mechanised columns thrusting their way along the coastal roads, but we had no time to form defensive positions that would stop the German advance.

No one who has fought against them could ever argue that the Germans were not great fighting troops, because they bloody well were. What's more, they were well trained, and their armour was far superior to anything we had in speed or firepower. General Wavell was still in overall command of the Imperial Army, installed in his headquarters hundreds of miles from the battle front in Egypt, while we poor sods in the front line were doing our best to hold the Germans; and I'm ashamed to have to admit it, but all the German equipment was better than ours, and Rommel's field tactics were far more imaginative than those of our field commanders, because he simply kept up with his army and planned his strategy as the battles developed, and didn't have to take orders from headquarters staff officers, safely tucked up hundreds of miles away from the fighting in Cairo.

On the other hand, our blokes had never had to deal with armoured tanks that our two-pounder anti-tank shells bounced off, nor the tracked field gun lorries and troop transporters that brought artillery and infantry right up to the fighting line, troops fresh and eager to take on us poor, bloody, foot-sore, battle-weary, dog-tired infantry of the retreating Imperial Army. So you see, even with all that experience our lads had gained from fighting the Italians, we couldn't stop the Jerries knocking ten bells out of us with the modern equipment they'd been supplied with, set against our pathetic obsolescent rubbish, much of which was left over from the First World War. Surely it must have been obvious to those in authority that as soon as the Germans came into the fighting line General Wavell's army didn't have the tanks and guns to match the German Panzers, nor an on-the-spot field commander to match General Erwin Rommel's tactics. We were outmanoeuvred to such an extent that we were given order after order to make what was termed 'tactical withdrawals'. In other words full-scale bloody retreats.

It was during one of these 'withdrawals' that our company was ordered to stay behind as a rear guard. The spot that had been chosen for us to 'stop the enemy in his tracks' was behind some small sand dunes near the road, between Sidi-Rezekh and Sallum, just inside the Egyptian border. Our company commander was ordered to hold the ground and the road for as long as possible; but it was obvious to the greenest of us we had come under the military term for such foolhardy ventures as being 'expendable'.

There was no obvious way out: we were literally in the open and it was quite plain that as soon as the Jerries came across us on the road, they would call down their Stuka dive bombers to soften us up, before making a pincer movement, and come round either side of our positions with the Panzers firing their 50mm shells and machine guns, while the half-track vehicles disgorged their infantry for a full-scale frontal assault, to give us hell. It was good tank country. We were supposed to be acting as a 'covering infantry company' to a battery of two-pounder anti-tank guns that had been dug in by Royal Artillery gunners behind and to the left and right of the sand dune.

We infantrymen had dug slit trenches – they were just holes, really, that the soft sand kept running back into. We cleaned our rifles and sten guns, had a light meal and a mug of tea, and while some of the older soldiers slept, we new lads watched the gunners busily trying to hide all traces of their position, before we all settled down to await the next episode of the forthcoming drama *Death in the Desert Sands*.

As the day wore on, the last of our retreating forward troops passed by our position, except, that is, for a few Australians and New Zealanders, who chose to stay behind with us. The noise of gunfire that had been drawing closer all day suddenly ceased altogether; you might say it was as silent as a grave. Our sergeant was on his rounds all the time and he'd pop his head over the slit trenches and whisper: 'Are you two all right? Keep your eyes open lads. I know you're tired, but don't drop off to sleep, because if you do, you could wake up and find yourselves dead. You'll be easy meat for the Jerries, just keep alert, and when they come we'll be ready for 'em.' He'd then go off to the other trenches, one after another, to make sure his soldiers were ready for whatever was to befall them.

'I told you he was a good'un,' John whispered to me. 'He's got character and guts, that sergeant has, and what's more, he knows his men won't let him down.' With that John reached into his tunic pocket and pulled out a pack of cards. 'Fancy playing a hand of cards, Bert?' he asked me.

'No, I damn well don't,' I replied. So we just sat in our hole, looking down the desert road. It was a beautiful night with the heaven full of twinkling stars – you know how those nights are out there in North Africa. The heat of the day had gone and there was a little bit of breeze before it began to get cold; everything that was a couple of feet off the ground was silhouetted against the skyline as plain as it would be in daylight – before long some poor soul, fully aware he was a living target, had got to come into the range of the guns. It reminded me of the rifle ranges in fairgrounds, where the little targets keep going round in a continuous chain, the only difference being they didn't know they were going to be killed.

I suppose we had been waiting about most of the night before we heard a faint rumbling on the road. It was difficult to judge how far away it was, except for the fact it was getting louder and closer. There could be no doubt as to what it was: Panzers. Our company captain soon had his binoculars trained on them and muttered, 'Armoured scout cars followed by Panzers, with troop-transported infantry in support coming up behind. Don't fire till I give the order, and make sure every shot counts.'

That was the last order he gave before we heard the Stuka dive bombers; the blitzkrieg on our positions had begun.

After the dive bombers had left the scene (they hadn't done too much damage) the scout cars came gingerly along the road trying to draw our fire; they knew that at least some of us must be waiting for them, somewhere among the bomb holes left by the Stuka dive bombers. They hadn't met any opposition yet, but they were expecting it. The anti-tank guns were still intact but in those days they were obsolete two-pounders, and unless the Jerry Panzers were virtually on top of them, they were pretty ineffective against their armour. But the gunners knew their job and the guns were well dug in. They didn't have the range to be effective, so they had to let the Jerries get almost on top of them before they could open up. As soon as the gunners let off their first salvo, the Jerries let fly with everything they had.

When they opened fire, it was concentrated on our two-pounder gun. Soon all the anti-tank guns had been destroyed and all the gunners killed or wounded. We infantry had been drawn up in a semi-circle round the guns, and we let rip with our sten guns and rifles at the scout cars and the mechanised troop transports, so their infantry got a real pasting as they got off the lorries, and they took a lot of casualties. But the Jerry tanks came on and

Palletised cargo awaiting shipment, London docks in the 1970s. (Author's collection)

raked the whole area good and proper with their machine guns, and when John and I looked around, we found ourselves to be the only two left alive in our section – that is except for a few wounded. We didn't know what to do, not really. We had been drilled to take orders, not to think for ourselves. But it was obvious that if we didn't want to be killed or taken prisoner, and the Jerries wouldn't be in a mood to take prisoners with the losses they'd just suffered, we had to get away as fast and as far from the road as we possibly could. John suggested we should move in a semi-circle to bring ourselves back on to the road about 5 miles to the east of our present position. He reckoned the mauling we had just given their infantry would make them a bit more cautious and slow their advance down, and to top that we would also be making for our own lines. So we set off, picking up an extra couple of water bottles, some food and some hand grenades on our way. I had a Lee Enfield rifle and John got hold of a sten gun and more ammunition, which he said was more than heavy enough for us to lug about in that terrain. We didn't want too much gear, he said, but we wanted enough to get us out of trouble if we should get lumbered while on our way.

It was a very shrewd move on his part, as it turned out. We had been foot-slogging over the ruddy sand for the best part of a couple of hours, and if you have ever marched over that desert sand you'll know exactly what I mean, it drains the very life blood out of you. We were having a wroth off at each other every now and again, cursing each other when we fell down, when quite suddenly John stopped and stood as still as a statue, and I followed his example.

'Can you hear that engine noise?' he said.

'No,' I replied.

'Then you must have cloth ears. It's a Jerry scout car.'

'How can you tell?' I asked him.

When he replied he sounded agitated. 'It's the engine noise, you stupid sot,' he said. 'I'm a mechanic by trade. I know the sound of different types of engines.'

It was impossible for me to tell how many vehicles there were, on account of my not being able to hear the engine noises at all. But it seemed plausible to me that there should be vehicles about, after all we couldn't have been very far from the road. After we had been standing listening for a short time, the noise slowly died away until it was no longer audible, so we marched on.

By nightfall we must have covered several miles and as it began to get cooler, John suggested that we get ourselves a few hours sleep. 'Dig a 'ole in the sand, get in it, and cover yourself with the sand, or you'll be frozen to death during the night. The sand will help to keep the cold night air off of you.' I did as he said and covered myself with sand up to my shoulders, he did the same, and we slept until dawn.

When we woke up it was just beginning to get warm, so we opened a tin of bully beef (corned beef) which we ate with a few dry biscuits. We had drunk some of our water when John jumped up with a start.

'What's up John?' I gasped.

'Listen,' he said, pointing in what I thought must be the direction of the road. 'That engine noise – it's a ruddy tank, a Panzer.'

I stood transfixed for several seconds, listening. But I couldn't hear any engine noise. 'No, it can't be,' I said. 'They wouldn't send a tank out here, would they?'

'Who knows what they might do, or for what reason – there's a war on,' he said. 'Do you think they might have got wind there's one of those Long Range Desert Groups (LRDG) operating in this area?'

'It could be that, or maybe they're testing this ground to find out if it's fit to fight tank battles on, just in case they have to retreat back along the road, John,' I suggested.

John sat down and was silent for some time before he answered. 'I don't think it's a matter of finding if this is suitable tank-fighting country: they'd know that already. I reckon they must have noticed our tracks in the sand leading out here and have come to investigate them. It could be there is a LRDG operating in this area, or Laycock's commando unit. The Jerries would have a special reason for wanting to kill or capture any of them. They've been set up to operate behind enemy lines and attack road convoys, airfield and arms dumps. Yes, there could be a LRDG section or a commando unit somewhere around here.'

It was then, quite suddenly, that a Panzer came into view from behind a sand dune. 'Christ,' I yelled in surprise. 'Where did that soddin' thing come from?'

'I've been telling you there's a bloody tank about, you numb-skulled idiot,' John shouted. 'It's a good job we've seen it before the tank crew have seen us.' Then he said, 'Look, those footmarks of ours are standing out like a bandaged index finger on the hand of a concert pianist in the Royal Albert Hall. We'd better do something about them before the tank crew get their gun sights on the pair of us.' And with that he took off his shirt and ran back over our tracks for some 100 yards (91m). Then, swinging his shirt over the soft sand, he started to obliterate our footprints. When I saw what he was doing, I followed his example, and we retreated round a sand dune, leaving our old tracks coming to a dead end. It was a shrewd move, the logic of which I quickly came to understand.

'That was a bright idea, John,' I told him.

'Yes,' he answered. 'I picked that one up from an old Indian trick I saw used years ago in a Tom Mix cowboy film, but they did it with brushwood. The trouble is, there's not too many trees in this desert, is there, or haven't you noticed? Clever though just the same, isn't it?'

John quickly sized up our situation. 'Let's get up on to the ridge of a sand dune, in that way we'll keep a birds-eye view of that Panzer now it's come into view,' he said. So we clambered up the loose sand on to its ridge and waited for the soddin' thing to show itself, and when it did finally creep into view, it stopped at the very spot our footmarks ended.

'Those sots have been following our tracks,' said John. I bet they think we will lead them to where there are more troops. They're after our blood, the devils. They don't give anything up. They're bloody good soldiers, those Germans. But I wonder what they're thinking now; perhaps they think we've done the Indian rope trick.'

'Blimey, John,' I said. 'What are we going to do?'

John turned his head and glared at me; there was hatred in his eyes. 'What are we going to do? Well old mate,' he said, 'they've chased us, now it's our turn; they're out looking for trouble – now they've found it. I'm going to knock that soddin' Panzer out and I'm going to kill the lot of them that's inside it. That's what I'm going to do.'

'You're going to do what? Knock that bloody tank out with a rifle, a sten gun and half a dozen hand grenades? You must be some sort of raving lunatic or something!'

John's face broke into a crafty smile, and he winked. Then he said, 'You've got to admit that we can't outrun 'em or out shoot 'em, right?'

'Right,' I said.

'Then that leaves just two alternatives: on the one hand we can fight it out here, where we are vulnerable and could in all probability get ourselves killed; but on the other we could surrender and take our chances they won't shoot us, right?'

'Yes, you're right,' I replied.

'Well,' he went on, 'I'm not fighting it out with that soddin' thing in the open, and I've no intention of spending the rest of the war in a German prison camp, so whether you like it or not our only chance of getting clear of that mechanised contraption down there is to knock it out. That Panzer is a German PzKpfw Mark III. The Mark III has got a crew of five men, so what we are going to do is immobilise it first, then we'll be able to pick any of them off with our rifles as they try to get out, because they will have to come out sometime to find out why the bloody thing won't move. We've got the advantage because we know why it's stationary, and don't forget, we've got water and food out here, enough to last us several days. And when the sun gets on the metal of that bloody thing, they'll have to have fresh air and try to get out – they can't win.'

'Well mate, we'll never get away with it. Nobody in our position would be stupid enough to take on a tank. You know yourself, that thing carries a 50mm gun and two machine guns,' I tried to reason with him.

'You mean you won't have a go at it,' John spat on the ground then said, 'I'll bet you £10 to a pinch of salt I can do the job on my own.'

'If you think you can do it, John, then you're on,' I told him.

We each spat into our palms and shook hands to seal the bet. Then he said, 'I may need a bit of help.'

'That's all right,' I replied.

'You're not going to bet me for a pinch of salt though, are you?'

'No, I'll lay you odds of two to one you can't do it.'

'I'll have a fiver,' said John, and we shook hands again.

'Then let's get this right: that's my £10 against your fiver, right?'

'Yes, that's it then,' he said. 'Now let me explain: as you already know, I used to work in a garage till I was conscripted into the army. The foreman of our workshop knew a few of the villains in the dock cafes, who used to arrange for some of the goodies to fall off the backs of lorries taking freight into and out of the East India, Millwall and West India docks. On some occasions police cars would be stationed near the dock entrances to follow drivers suspected of off-loading goods to places other than their rightful destinations. When our foreman was given the tip, he would send a couple of us apprentices to where the police cars were stationed; we would play ball behind the police cars, make out we were picking it up, then shove a handful of rag waste, attached to a piece of string, up the car's exhaust pipe. When the police got sight of their quarry, they would try to start the car – of course it wouldn't because the exhaust was blocked up. They would always do the same thing: get out of the car and look at the engine, scratch their heads, get back in the car and the car would start. The reason: we had pulled the plug of rag waste out of the exhaust, by which time the lorry driver had delivered his odd packages and was back on his bona fide route. Now, you watch this,' he said.

We had pulled our shirts back on after covering our tracks in the sand; John now quickly took his off again and part filled it with sand. 'When that soddin' Panzer comes to the end of our tracks, it will stop for one of the crew to get out and have a look around to see if there are any other tracks about. As soon as it stops and one of them gets out, all I want you to do is give me some covering fire to draw it over here. Now, as soon as it comes round the back of that dune, I'm away.'

The Panzer moved slowly over the sand between the dunes as John crept out of the sight of the tank crew, round the base of another sand dune towards it, just as he had learnt to do as an apprentice. He was surreptitiously heading towards it as they, unbeknown to them, were travelling towards him. Then when the Panzer got level with him, on the opposite side of the sand dune, John ran up to the dune ridge, where he waited until the tank was 10ft away from him. Then he jumped off the top of the dune, slid down the other side and, running up behind the tank, he put some sand inside the shirt and rammed it into the exhaust pipe. Having done that, he ran back up the side of the dune and quickly jumped for cover over the top. Fortunately, none of the tank crew had seen him. He made his way back to my side as fast as his little hairy legs would carry him.

The Panzer, on the other hand, was still moving slowly forward, but all of a sudden its engine started to splutter – then the tank stopped dead in its tracks. Well, I thought, at least he learnt something useful while he was doing his apprenticeship as a car mechanic; he's bunged up the exhaust and the engine can't breathe – this has become interesting, that's shortened the odds a bit, the cheeky sot.

Now I've never been able to fathom out why the tank commander wasn't in his turret, because if he had been it's doubtful if John could ever have got close enough to that Panzer to have bunged his shirt up its exhaust. But John came back and lay down beside me, bursting out laughing. 'There you are,' he said. 'I doubt if you have ever seen a Panzer suffering from a severe bout of induced restrictive constipation before, have you?' And I had to admit I hadn't. Then John said:

'Here we are then, on a sand dune, and there they are, in their tank. We've got two .303 Lee Enfield rifles, a sten gun and some hand grenades; they've got one 50mm gun, two machine guns and their side arms (quite possibly hand pistols). We're out in the open and mobile; they are in their tank and static. I stand a good chance of making ten nicker out of you.'

'Yes, you do,' I told him.

With that he slid back down the side of the dune and worked his way round on to the opposite side of the tank. Then he waved his vest at me to show he had taken up his position. *Sod him*, I thought, *if he wants to take ten quid off of me, he's going to have to bloody well earn it. I'll leave it to him to work out how he intends to finish them off.* It was then that the tank's hatch began to open and a bloke climbed out. They obviously didn't suspect somebody had stopped their tank for them, but as the bloke who had climbed out of the turret jumped clear of the tank, I saw John level his rifle and heard the Lee Enfield crack out. I think, on reflection, the bullet must have struck the German in the shoulder, because he spun round before he hit the sand, where he just lay quite still near the tank's tracks. Then another member of the tank crew came out of the hatch and John shot him, too. I could almost sense what the other three blokes in the tank were thinking, 'How many of them are there out there? Where are the enemy? Who are the enemy? What weapons have the enemy got? And why won't this bloody tank work?'

From what they had seen of the footsteps in the sand, they knew there were at least two of us, but what they didn't know was whether they had they been led into an ambush. They'd obviously followed our tracks for quite some way, determined to get us either dead or alive. Now the survivors were stuck in their tank with a 50mm gun and two machine guns and no visible targets to use them on. What must have been most obvious to them was that they were stationary and we (the enemy) were mobile; we knew where they were but they didn't know where we were; they would be aware we would know a Panzer had a crew of five and that they had already lost two men, and if any of them tried to get out of the tank they'd suffer the same fate as their mates.

I called across to John, who was settled behind a ridge on an adjourning dune, 'What do we do now?'

'We've just got to sit and wait for them to make the next move, that's all,' he shouted back.

All of a sudden I began to laugh, God knows why. I began to laugh like a village idiot. I thought, *No one will ever believe this, I mean, what sort of a lunatic is it that will bet his mate he could knock out a tank armed with a rifle, a sten gun and a few hand grenades – and for a paltry ten quid. What's more he's as good as damn near done it. He's got the worst bit of it over, now all he's got to do is to finish them off.* I was still laughing when I saw John trotting from the side of a dune, on the opposite side to where the Panzer was, and come running up to me round the back of the tank, panting and sweating like an old bulldog laying in the sun.

'That's damn well fixed 'em, hasn't it?' he said, gasping for breath. 'Now they can't move the Panzer can they, and if they want to fight they'll have to come out here to do it. The only problem we've got is if they see anything move out here, then they'll open fire with that 50mm gun of theirs but every time they do that it will be one shell less – that's unless they get us with a lucky shot, of course. I don't know how many shells those tanks carry, but in the end if they don't get us first, they're going to have to get out of that oversized tin can they're in and try fighting it out with us in the open using their small arms; either that or surrender. Knowing those bastards, they won't surrender, at least not now they think they've got our army on the run and they think they're going to beat us all the way back to Suez. If they knew how many of us there are out here though, they would take their chances and get out of that contraption and take us on. It's lucky for them they don't know, because if they do try to get out for a scrap, I'll shoot them down like I did their mates. Now I've got to go back to my niche on the ridge of that sand dune. If they should decide to come out whilst I'm on my way back over there, whatever happens, don't let any of them get their hands on that machine gun in the turret, because as sure as they do, that'll be curtains for the pair of us. One of them will be able to pin us down while his mates get out: they'll soon twig on to what we've done, then they'll get back inside that tank and then I doubt if even God will be able to help us.' And with the last words of his speech, he slid down the side of the dune and made his way back to his chosen perch, the same way as he had come, to await the next move of the tank's occupants.

We sat there for hours, trying to keep out of the rays of the sun, each of us squatting on the ridge of our sand dune. It was hot enough sitting where we were. Christ knows how the tank crew were faring, the interior of the tank must have been like an oven: without the engine running there was no way they could cool the cabin down. So we sat waiting and watching, both with our separate thoughts, until all of a sudden a head popped up through the turret and as suddenly disappeared again. Then a head and shoulders popped up and once again dipped quickly out of sight.

John yelled across at me from his sand castle dune, 'For Christ's sake shoot the next Jerry who tries to get out of that soddin' tank and into the turret, and scarper as fast as you can – they're trying to draw our fire to get a fix on our position so they can take a pot-shot at us with that 50mm gun. I'm going to move further round to the next dune; then I'll be able to shoot anyone who tries to get out, right.'

Then, after giving me those instructions, John disappeared from his perch on the dune ridge and made his way to an adjoining sand dune.

The Germans in the tank then began to try drawing our fire by a bit of subterfuge: they'd rolled up a cloth garment which they'd pressed into a helmet and with a wooden pole they slowly pushed the helmet up through the hatch cover into the turret; I have to admit I really thought it was one of them trying to creep up into the turret so I loosed off a shot and slid off the dune as fast as I could. I was just in time, because the next thing that happened was a shell from the 50mm gun hit the side of my dune, and when it exploded it caused a deluge of sand to descend over a wide area. I was almost smothered but I hastily made my way to the next sand dune, and with all the speed I could muster, I scrambled up to its top, just in time to see bullets from the tank's turret machine guns rake the whole length of the ridge I'd just vacated. The sand on the ridge was dancing, just like you see rain dancing on a country millpond in

England. *Blimey,* I thought, *that German gunner's pretty nifty with those machine guns.* Then I heard the distinctive sound of a rifle shot. The twin machine guns stopped firing as I made my way over to where John was lying, face down on the top of a sand dune, with his legs stretched apart just as he'd been trained to do, and with his rifle aimed at the tank's turret. When I got beside him he simply said:

'That leaves just two of them now, Bert. I wonder how much petrol they've got left in that tank?'

'Why?' I asked.

'I've never driven a tank,' he replied. 'I've driven cars, vans, heavy lorries and diesel cranes; but I've never driven a tank. There's no point in us marching out of here when this fiasco's over, if we can ride out, now is there? But if we can't get that tank all in one piece by getting them out of there today, then I'll have to go down there tonight and blast them out of it with these grenades, whether I like it or not. In the mean time we'd better split up.'

'All right,' I replied. 'We'll see what's got to be done tonight to shift them out of that tank. You go and get some kip if you can. There are only two of 'em left, so I doubt if they will try anything rash. If they do make a move, I'll give you a shout, okay?'

With those final few words, John moved off to another sand dune and was soon fast asleep. He had most of the work to do that night, so it was only fair that he should get some kip first. Anyway it was up to him, and it was he who had made the wager. However, while John slept I sat sentinel and kept a close watch on the tank's turret, making sure they didn't try any tricks. But they must have had it in their minds to do what we were doing, waiting for the cover of the night. I doubt if they realised that they couldn't win this fight – anyway they were too arrogant after their victories even to contemplate defeat – but John had them at checkmate even if they didn't know it. He was a born soldier, John was. To see him at work you would never have thought he'd been born and raised in London's East End. You'd have thought he'd never done anything else but soldiering; but soldiering came as second nature to him, that boy from Stepney's slum community that lived a hand-to-mouth existence on the banks of the River Thames.

However, I sat watching that bloody tank until I was cross-eyed, not daring to take a break from keeping it under surveillance, not even for one second, but it wasn't until about an hour before nightfall that things began to happen. It started when the hatch of the tank began to rise, and as it did a head began to emerge. I loosed off a round at it with my rifle because I didn't fancy taking a chance on letting one of them getting his hands on the twin machine guns. But I quickly realised I was too late and threw myself backwards off the dune just as the machine guns sent a hail of bullets into the area I'd just vacated. *Christ,* I thought, *he nearly got me that time.*

John was awake like a shot when he heard the firing, and was poised on his sand dune when I looked across to where I knew he was, with his rifle levelled at the tank. I jog-trotted over to his location.

'It's all right, John,' I assured him. 'I think one of them was just trying to find out if we are still about. You'd better try to get back to sleep.'

'No, I don't think so,' he replied. 'The sun will be going down before too long and I've been thinking. Why haven't they taken another shot at us with that 50mm gun of theirs? You'd have thought they would – after all we've had them bogged down here all day and nobody has come out here looking for them as yet, have they?' Then he said, 'You'd better get your head down, Bert, otherwise you may be too tired to move on when this pantomime is over. You'd better find another place to sleep while it's still warm – it'll get cold tonight as soon as the sun goes down and so you won't get any kip then. Go on, away with you.'

'Yes, okay,' I replied, and toddled off to another dune, climbed up to a spot nearest to its ridge where I had a good view of the tank, and almost immediately dropped of into an uneasy sleep.

It must have been a couple of hours later that I was woken up by a hell of a shindig going on down by the tank. John, it seems, had decided to put an end to our drama, and he'd gone down to the tank from off the top of his dune to finish the job off. I could see him down by the tank: he'd fixed his bayonet on to his rifle (they were those long bayonets those days) and it was glittering in the last rays of the sun. He'd obviously crept up behind the tank and chucked a hand grenade into the turret. There was a hell of an explosion as the ammunition inside ignited and the tank's turret flew up in the air and crash-landed about a hundred feet away from the tank.

It was quite obvious that the last two crewmen could not have survived the blast. John turned round to where I was watching and raised his rifle above his head. He started to run up the side of the sand dune towards me, and had got about half way when two shots rang out. Slowly John's legs began to buckle under him and he sank to his knees and fell face down on to the sand. *Jesus Christ*, I thought, *where did those soddin' shots come from.* Then it dawned on me: it had to be one of those blokes we'd thought we'd killed earlier on in the day. One of them must still be alive. I ran down to John's side, grabbed the sten gun that he had slung over his shoulder and, running round the tank, I sprayed the bodies that were lying on the sand with bullets. What had amazed me most was that when the tank had exploded it hadn't killed whoever it was that had fired the shots. But after I'd sprayed the bodies I fixed my bayonet before I walked over to where they were lying, just in case any one of them was still alive, to make sure this time they were all dead. Then I ran to where John was lying; there was a dark red bloodstain spreading over the back of his khaki singlet. I rolled him over on to his back and as I did he opened his eyes.

'Did I get the lot of them?' he asked, then. 'Did I win my wager?'

'Yes, John, you sure did,' I replied. 'But how am I going to get you out of here?'

'You won't move me from here, Bert,' he replied. 'You'd better find a shovel. There'll be one in the tank's tool kit.'

'Don't be silly, old mate,' I said. 'I'll think of something.'

'No you won't,' he said. 'I've had it. This is one wager you've lost and won't ever have to pay out on. You can have this bet on me.' And he died, where he'd fallen, on the sand.

Bert continued, 'There are quite a few blokes who have been awarded a Victoria Cross for doing half of what John did that day in the desert, all those years ago.'

'So why didn't he get a VC?' Bert was asked.

'Because,' he replied, 'you're the first people I've ever told this story to.'

'Why is that?' George said.

'Because I never thought anybody would ever believe me. But you can take my word that what I've just told you is the absolute truth.'

With those last words Bert stood up and walked over to the transit shed doorway, looked out on to the quay, then turned and walked back. There were tears on his cheeks that were noticed by the other dockers. Before anyone had a chance to make a remark that would embarrass him, George said: 'I see it's still raining, Bert. There's no point in us sitting about here. Come on, I'll take you up to the dock pub and treat you to a pint of beer. I've really worked myself up to a thirst in that desert, among the sand dunes.' And with those last few words they each slid their dockers' hooks in their belts, pulled their coats over their shoulders, and walked out of the transit shed doorway on to the quay and into the pouring rain.

In Conclusion

The ship's gang had been silenced by Bert's tale. They sat for some minutes spellbound as George and Bert walked off along the dock quay, heading for the public house known to all dock workers as 'The Top Canteen'. Then:

'That was a yarn, wasn't it?' said one of the gang known as 'Brains', simply because he had very little idea of how to use the one he'd got. 'I've never heard Bert talk so much; do you believe him? Well, I damn well don't, nor about the Germans landing the way they did.'

Terry stood up. He folded his *Daily Worker* newspaper, slid it into his pocket, then he turned round to glare at the speaker: 'What part of Bert's tale don't you believe? It can't be the bit about his gambling habit, because as you know full well he doesn't gamble. What's more neither do I. Perhaps you don't believe he was in the Imperial Army and served in the desert campaign in North Africa, but we all know he did. Don't you think his mate John was capable of destroying a German tank on his own? Well, perhaps you'll believe him now when I tell you a commando officer by the name of Michael Alexander, operating behind the German lines in the desert near El-Alamein in 1942, with other lay-force commandoes, did just that – all on his own. Now I'll tell you what Bert has just done, without his knowing it. He's got a burden of guilt off of his mind. He obviously hasn't been able to forgive himself for what he considers was his fault – accepting a wager that got his mate John killed. Guilt, for the benefit of you "ragged-arsed, bone-headed, wage slaves", is construed by psychoanalysts as being "a sense of wrong-doing"; it's an emotional, mental and nervous affliction involving internal mental conflict. Such mental conditions arise out of real or imagined contravention of social standards in either act or thought. For your further edification, guilt can also lead to repression or aggression within the mind. In Bert's case he was lucky, because aggression is a safety valve of the mental processes, and he has been able to release that aggression physically on the heads of numbskulls like you, when the urge takes hold of him. On the other hand, regression is something most people cannot deal with. They tend to retreat into themselves. Doctors generally refer to this illness as depression, and they prescribe drugs to help alleviate its symptoms when they should be referring the patient to a psychologist. Many people with this category of mental illness commit suicide. Bert will be a different man after today's verbal eruption, you'll see.' So he was, too.

However, Terry continued, 'About the Germans landing an army in Libya. Don't you think it was one of those odd coincidences during the 1939–45 War that a powerful enemy such as Germany was allowed to land troops almost unopposed in North Africa, to take up a cudgel for a defeated ally and continue battles without any effective opposition? Think about it, because that's what the Germans actually did when they landed in Libya. German ships had crossed the Mediterranean Sea, loaded with troops, tanks, ammunition and other military equipment, and were allowed to organise themselves and make advances of hundreds of miles before an effective resistance was organised against them.'

'I've never thought about it,' one of the ship's gang said. 'But I suppose you and your Russian communist mates have.'

'Before I continue with my assessment of the North African campaign, let me put you straight on one thing, you idiot,' said Terry. 'I haven't got any communist mates; Russia isn't and never has been a communist state. The Soviet Union is an amalgamation of socialist republics governed from Moscow; just as America is fifty capitalist countries governed from Washington DC. It's true that Russian political policy is centralised under a virtual dictator, Stalin; but it's also true that the American states are governed by a federal government controlled under an elected president, as are the four countries of the United Kingdom that are governed from London; and the six states of Australia that are controlled from Canberra, and so on. There is very little difference in the form of political control, which is administered by bureaucrats. What are different are the political ideologies behind the bureaucracies, and the distribution of wealth among the peoples who create that wealth. Right. Now let me get back to what I was explaining to you about my assessment of the German involvement in North Africa.

'I believe the Germans were enticed by the British to land an army in Libya. This was done simply as a way of draining German resources in armaments and men away from Europe, and a possible second attempt at invading the British Isles. Churchill's War Cabinet, through their possession of the Enigma machine, and with the aid of code-breakers at Bletchley Park (or Station X as it was known), would have been advised on German strategy in the Mediterranean war zones, and no doubt advised by British Intelligence Services, the British War Cabinet decided to tie up German resources on the African continent as a means of weakening their position in their attack against Russia and us in the European theatre of war. Our desert army, either in their advances or their retreats, kept the Germans bogged down in the desert, while our aircraft, submarines and surface ships sank the German supply vessels, and shot down their supply aircraft. This tactic bought the Allies time while they built up enough military strength for an invasion of Sicily and Italy, and as a diversion to a full-scale invasion of Europe through France via Normandy. That's why I think a German army was encouraged to land in North Africa.'

'I don't believe a word of that,' said Brains.

'Well,' replied Terry. 'You're having a brain constructed out of pomegranates seeds and the mental capability of a rotten apple. I wouldn't expect you to understand anything that's entirely logical, now would I?'

With that last remark the whole gang burst into raucous laughter. Well, if you'd seen the look on poor Brains' face, what would you have done?

TALE 4

OLD PERCY'S REVENGE

Now I'm fully aware that this introduction isn't what most readers expect to see when they begin reading a tale, but I'm of the opinion that this particular tale will have lost some of its substance if the historic facts relating to its authenticity are not recorded. That is an explanation as to the facts relating to the industrial background that shows the psychopathic indifference of employers and trade and general worker union negotiators, in their joint dealings with manpower problems in industrial blue-collar work environments.

It's with this thought in mind, therefore, that the first paragraphs of this tale are written specifically to enlighten readers as to why old dockers and stevedores could be found during the 1960s and 1970s idling the final years of their lives away in pubs and clubs around the dock areas, where they had lived all their lives, with the exception of those years they were absent fighting wars against their Majesties' enemies in theatres of war around the world, waiting patiently in a diminishing queue to meet their maker.

Dockers and stevedores, beginning with men over sixty-eight years of age, had been forced to relinquish their jobs in the docking industry by the National Dock Labour Board (LDLB), when the National Joint Council (NJC) for the Port Transport Industry, an industrial joint employer and trade and general workers union negotiating organisation, had decided to have the older members of the workforce in those docks that employed registered dock workers as under the Dock Workers (Regulation of Employment) Act 1947. This was an exercise in enforced retirement that began in 1960 with the passing by Parliament of the Dock Workers (Pension) Act, which culminated in 1963 with the payment (for those men who had contributed into the Dock Workers Voluntary Pension Fund) of a lump sum of £100 and 10s per week for life.

Among those men to be removed from the NDLB register in the Port of London under this directive was Old Percy, who on having his name and therefore his livelihood taken away from him by the NDLB, got himself another job to subsidise his paltry old age pension, and worked on until he was seventy-three years of age. That was before the war wounds he had received in the service of thankless governments and injuries he had sustained in the docks over many years finally caught up with him. Only then did he pack it in.

However, Old Percy wasn't without a sense of humour, for as he so often put it when asked why he had retired, he'd simply reply in those memorable cricketing terms: 'I retired hurt.'

To be denied access to employment in the docks, where he had worked for forty-seven years, since his discharge from the army in 1918 as unfit for further military service due

The author's father, young Percy
Charles Bradford, France 1916.
(Author's collection)

to wounds inflicted on him during the Battle of the Somme, was an event that had been
a cultural shock to Old Percy – he had never been unemployed since he left school at age
twelve. But for a number of years after his enforced retirement, he often met up with his
former workmates and army comrades and had a social 'pint or two of beer' with them, as
they reminisced both about their working days in the docks and less often (unless they were
half drunk and the pain of their experiences on the South African veldt, in the trenches of
northern France, or some other better to be forgotten battlefield, got the better of them)
about the carnage they had witnessed and been party to during the dreadful years of those
distant wars, now lost to history.

It was during one of these gatherings in a local working man's club that I stupidly decided
to call in to see my workmates. The 'boys of the old brigade' were gathered in strength – well
those that were left of them that is – after having attended the funeral of an old workmate and
comrade. And although they appeared to be in a jovial mood, it was obvious to me they were

simmering like magma beneath the laughter and at the drop of a hat they would explode in venomous rhetoric or even violent aggressive action, should any pretext or reason present itself; I'd seen it happen before in similar circumstances, when they had been much younger, 'bomb happy' from mental scarring from yesteryear's battles, and far more dangerous.

Having entered the lounge area of the working man's club and seen what was going on in there, I decided to beat a hasty retreat, and was about to go out through the swing doors by which means I had just entered that place, when a familiar voice called out: 'Don't you bloody disappear; come and buy me a drink, then you can do me a favour.'

I turned and, looking across the lounge, I saw Old Percy propped up in a bucket chair. He was holding a half-empty pint glass in his hand and was beckoning at me with his index finger to get him a refill. I cursed the old devil under my breath but dutifully made my way to the bar, bought a pint of beer and took it over to him.

'Why didn't you come straight over here?' he said. 'It's my turn to buy a round.'

'Oh!' I said in mock surprise. 'I thought so, but I'm not your son for nothing, you must remember, you've caught me like that before, often.'

Years of in-house training had taught me most of his tricks, although he still had a basketful more of them that he unleashed on unsuspecting fellow travellers, in as many unsuspecting ways. That's the reason I kept well clear of him when he was out and about in the community, loose and fancy-free, where I couldn't control his antics and where I knew he would take every advantage of my good nature that he could. I now waited in trepidation for his next demand. But God only knows why I ever allowed myself to let him order me into carrying out the sorts of favours and requests he constantly made on my time – the only excuse I can give is because he was my father, the belligerent old sot.

'What do you want now? I'm looking for Les and Don. They've promised to do a job for me,' I told him.

'They've been and gone; you won't find them now. They went off with some bloke to do a job for him. You'll have to see them at work in the Dock Labour Board compound tomorrow. Anyway, I want you to take me to Maidstone market; it's Tuesday today and there is something I need to do there,' he insisted.

As I had missed Les and Don, and couldn't do the job I had planned to get done, I reluctantly succumbed to his request, told him to get his coat and, pushing him in front of me, we made our way to my van and I drove him to Maidstone.

When we arrived in Maidstone, I drove to the market and I found a place to park. I couldn't help saying to myself under my breath, 'God only knows why I let myself get involved in Old Percy's idiosyncratic urges and ideas,' as I was instantly solicited by stallholders from all directions with the usual cries of, 'Do you want to buy this coat, Gov? 'Ere, try this hat, or these boots or these shoes?' All of which were being touted at 'half normal retail price, mate', although they never told one what the full price the article may have been.

Old Percy was in his element as we pushed our way through the streams of people, each of them desperately trying to go in a different direction, for they too were being chivvied and harassed by stallholders, and most of them appeared to be as desperate as we to escape the consequences of loitering too long on any one spot. After all, the price of standing still left them open to the pressure sales patter of determined vendors of non-returnable goods, as they had bellowed in their ears sales patter such as: 'Buy a coat Gov, you won't buy better gear anywhere. I'm bloody giving the stuff away as it is. I've got to be careful, it was only nicked yesterday; the coppers aren't on to me yet, but I've got to get rid of it today, before the owners twig on it's missing. I could be in prison by this time tomorrow. Come on Gov, be a sport, do me a favour, buy a coat.' And: 'Have your photo taken, mate. You only have to hold the monkey.' Then before one realises what is happening, a monkey is thrust into one's arms, and one is standing holding a miniature primate that clutches desperately to one's coat with its hands and feet, apparently trying to shield itself from the beastly photographer who is hell bent on subjecting the poor animal to further humiliation.

The scene at Maidstone market on this particular day was colourful, or perhaps it could better be described as picturesque. The stall area is situated on the west side of the River Medway, to the eastern side of the old stone bridge, and almost directly opposite All Saints church, which rises not too impressively above the ring road on the opposite shore of the river's steep bank.

The river itself meanders slowly through Maidstone town, and in the summer is serene with swans continuously dipping their heads in the water (as swans tend to have the habit of doing) and ducks diving beneath the water, searching for whatever ducks search for. Rowing boats hired from the boathouse keeper's yard on the opposite shore were haphazardly rowed up and down the river by people who come to spend a day in the county town of Kent on market day.

High on his dais, a policeman directs traffic to allocated parking places in the market car park. The market stalls, arranged in blocks between the covered market and the river, are ablaze with various colours: men in t-shirts and short trousers; young girls and women traipsing about among the crowds, wearing mini-skirts that almost come up to their hips and flimsy blouses through which the curves of their bodies stood out in 3D outline. There were also farmers dressed in heavy tweed breeches, short-sleeved shirts and high riding boots; townsmen in tight-fitting trousers or shorts, with open-necked shirts and wearing sandals; elderly ladies, attired in long heavy frocks or skirts were prominent among the crowds, and highlighted the marked visible difference between the young and the old, between countrymen and townsmen.

All these people had come to the market to buy or sell produce from the surrounding countryside or factory-produced goods in all shapes and forms, but with an overwhelming emphasis on clothes – new or second-hand. There were stalls selling government surplus stores, stalls selling eggs and honey; others were hawking clocks and watches. If you could name whatever it was one wanted, there was sure to be some stallholder in the market who would be able to purchase or obtain by any means a way of acquiring it for one.

In the enclosed market, the cultured voice of an auctioneer could be heard running up the price of goods and chattels with: 'One pound; one pound and fifty pence; two pounds; who'll give me two-pound fifty? Two pounds then – going once, going twice; sold to number 21.' Such scenes were all part of market days in Maidstone. Every Tuesday, rain or shine.

I hadn't wanted to go to Maidstone market. I had more than enough work to do at home, but Old Percy had badgered me to take him. Now, when I come to think about it, I have the feeling it was a premonition he'd had. For he'd been most insistent on making this trip on this particular day, certainly for reasons I could not at the time comprehend.

As the morning wore on, and the shoving and pushing became more aggressive and intense, as ever more people crammed themselves among the stalls and on to the towpath and grassed banks of the Medway, Old Percy decided that it would be a good idea to buy a bag of fish and chips from the mobile fish and chip shop, then retreat on to the river bank and relax on a bench and eat them.

'Right,' Old Percy said. 'I'll get a seat by the river, you go and get the fish and chips.'

Of course, he didn't offer me any money to purchase the fish and chips, but he never had offered to pay before, so he wasn't going to break the habit of a lifetime just to please me – at least not if it was going to cost him any money. So, having bought our pieces of fish and chips, I made for the cast-iron gate that led from the market on to the river bank and I found him sitting on a wooden seat that was set facing the river, lost in thought as though mesmerised by the ripples on the water's surface. I'd never seen him in that pose before – never. It was a peaceful site he'd chosen to sit, watching the swans with their cygnets, gliding back and forth, slowly and without fuss. There were fishermen too, sitting as still as statues except for the occasional tug on their fishing lines, waiting and waiting. One wonders why they sit so patiently hour after hour, until one hears the tinkle of a bell that is attached to a small float, which bobs up and down on the water's surface and sends the fishermen into action. First one hears the purring of the reels ratchet, which sends buzzing sounds over the now rippling water as the almost silent struggle between life and death is fought out between fisherman and fish; between the hunter and the hunted; the killer and its victim.

It was then an extraordinary thing happened. We had finished eating our fish and chip lunch, and were looking down at the river's surface, when the growling of a dog made me turn in my seat. Behind us, on the other side of the seat, stood a large mongrel dog, with its teeth bared, obviously suggesting to us in its canine way that we should push off and sit somewhere else.

'Now Tommy, that's enough of that,' an elderly lady was saying. 'We haven't got a monopoly on this seat, you know. We only have it when we get here first.'

Old Percy didn't even bother to look over his shoulder, but said in his gruff voice: 'It's all right love, you come and sit down here, there's plenty of room on this seat for all of us.' It was as though he had been expecting her.

The old lady came round to the front of the seat and sat down. She must have been close to eighty-plus years of age, but by her features she had been, in her youthful days, a very beautiful woman. For even now, with grey wisps of curly hair erupting from beneath the sides of a French -tyle beret, puffing out like steam wafting from the sides of a boiling saucepan lid, and with her sharp grey-blue eyes that sparkled unusually bright for a woman of her age and with rosebud shaped lips that slightly parted when she smiled, she was still an impressive-looking woman.

She was, however, wearing an unbuttoned black coat over a black dress that came down almost to her ankles. She appeared to have no legs, as they were hidden under the dress, and a pair of black laced-up boots. The only other part of her anatomy that was exposed to the light of day, except for her head, was her hands, which were calloused from years of hard work and heavy toil. On her left hand she wore a thin wedding ring that had cut itself deeply into her skin. On the back of her hands the veins stood out like a ribbon of miniature blue mountains running across the sand-coloured desert of her skin. She sat on the seat bolt upright, with her dog at her feet. She was a person from a bygone age. It was as if she was a photograph taken from a history book – and for the first time in my life I actually felt humbled, for I suddenly realised: so was my dad, Old Percy.

'It's a lovely day, my dear,' he said to her. 'You must be very hot, wearing all those heavy togs?'

'Yes, it is rather warm,' she replied. 'But I like to dress up like this till June. Remember the old saying, "Never caste a clout till May is out".'

'Oh, yes! The very words my mother used to use,' he replied. 'You must come here quite often.' He pointed at the dog. 'The animal appears to think it has priority rights to this seat.'

'No, not very often,' she said. 'But this is the seat we do sit on when we come here. I live in a small flat over there.' She pointed across the river. 'And this is quite a long walk for me now, but my dog needs the exercise, so I come as often as I can.'

'Hum,' Old Percy grunted in reply.

'I see you are an old soldier of the Queen's Own Royal West Kent Regiment,' she said, and pointed at his lapel on which was displayed a regimental badge. 'My husband was in the Royal West Kent Regiment.'

'He was,' Old Percy said as though he already knew.

'Yes, he was in the regular army before the First World War,' she continued.

'So was I,' replied Old Percy.

'When were you in the army?'

'I joined the West Kents in Woolwich, June 1913, just a week before my seventeenth birthday, and seventeen days before the assassination in Sarajevo of Archduke Francis Ferdinand, heir to the Hapsburg thrones.'

'That's a coincidence,' she said. 'My husband joined the regular army in 1913, too. I don't remember which month.'

'Oh, yes,' said Old Percy.

The two of them sat in silence for some time, until the old lady suddenly said, 'My husband was killed in the Great War; it seems such a long time ago, most of the people of our time are dead, the young people today could never understand.'

'I haven't forgotten,' said Old Percy. 'I could never forget.'

'No. I don't suppose you ever could. What company were you in?'

'D Company, first battalion.'

'Oh! My husband was in D Company. Perhaps you knew him?'

'Perhaps I did,' said Old Percy. 'What was his name?'

'Atkins, hence my dog's name, Tommy. I call all my dogs Tommy to remind me of him.'

'Billy Atkins,' Old Percy blurted out.

'Yes, that's right – you do remember him. Did you know him well?'

'Yes, I got to know him very well.'

'He was a lovely man, my Billy was. He was always pleasant to everyone. People who knew him always said so.'

'Yes he was a good man in deed and word,' said Old Percy. 'He minded his own business, never asked a favour, but he was always ready to give anyone a hand if it was needed.'

'He would,' said the old lady.

'Yes, and he faced up to the terrible conditions in France with the best of them. No one in this country could ever understand just what those conditions were like; but I suppose Billy had the benefit of his religious ideology to sustain him.'

'Yes, he was a member of our chapel, and he always attended services when he was home on leave.'

'He was older than me,' Old Percy said. 'Two or three years older I think.'

'Yes, I suppose he would have been. He joined the army a few weeks after we were married – I was eighteen and he was twenty-one. He joined the army because he couldn't get a job; things were bad, we were told it was one of those economic recessions, there were thousands of men out of work, people were emigrating to Australia, New Zealand and Canada, anywhere they could escape away from the poverty in our towns and cities. But Billy and me, we were expecting our first baby and he was worried stiff. We could hardly afford to buy any food and we were well behind with our rent. Billy went out one day to find work; he had two pence in his pocket. He met a so-called friend of his, who took him into the Seven Greys public house for a pint of beer. There was a recruiting sergeant in the public bar, who talked Billy into taking the king's shilling, egged on by his "friend".'

'Yes, I remember Billy telling me,' Old Percy replied. 'The recruiting sergeant was paying Billy's friend 3*d* for every recruit he could get to sign up.'

Suddenly the old lady looked up at the clock on All Saints church, then stood up.

'Well I must be going now,' she said, 'but I've always come here on this day every year, *our* day, you know, mine and Billy's. Billy always joked about this place being a time capsule. The scenery is always the same, he would say. Through hundreds of years of English history this place has looked the same as it does today. People, they come and go, others follow them and in their turn they too go. These surroundings, they don't change very much; it's only the people that keep changing.' And she finally said, 'Yes, it's only the people.'

She then pushed a loose wisp of white hair back beneath her beret, and with a final 'come on Tommy' to her dog, walked slowly away down the towpath towards the cast-iron gates, back the way she had come, into the oblivion of history.

Old Percy stood up as she had turned to go and he nodded to her as she began to walk away. It was the only time I'd ever known him to do such a thing. Then he sat down and began to stare at the water. I thought he was watching the swans and the cygnets, until I noticed he had tears in the corners of his eyes, but I said not a word. I just sat and waited, and it was some time before he spoke to me.

'An odd thing, don't you think, that I should meet Billy Atkins' widow today,' he said.

'A chance in a thousand million, if it was an off-chance I should say,' was my reply.

'It was sixty-five years ago today Billy Atkins was killed,' he said, in a melancholic way. 'We had become close friends, although Billy was a few years older than me. He treated me more like I was his younger brother; sort of wet-nursed me a bit. The Great War started on 4 August 1914 when Britain declared war on Germany, while we were still in training, but by November the Old Contemptible of the British Expeditionary Force (BEF) had almost been wiped out. There was a scramble by the high command to get more infantry over to France to stop the German advance. So our battalion, the 1st Queen's Own Royal West Kent Regiment, was sent from Dublin to northern France, in December 1914. We went to the front line almost immediately and were in the trenches on Christmas Day. Billy spent a lot of his time keeping me out of trouble. We were both marksmen (snipers), but I couldn't resist taking pot-shots at the Jerry trenches. Billy kept telling me not to stop in the same place after firing a couple of rounds, or one of their snipers would get a shot in at me. In the battles our battalion fought in during 1914–16, those were on the Aisne where we had dozens of men killed, Hill 60 where we lost almost all our regular officers including Major Joslin, Captain Tuff, Lieutenants Payton, Walker and Job, D Company came off Hill 60 with one sergeant and nine of us privates, the second battle of Ypres, the Somme and God only knows how many skirmishes in between. Billy and I were inseparable, be it on the front line, the support trenches or in reserve. Billy wasn't that much older than me really, but just that much older to be more mature in the way he thought about and did things. When the soddin' officers began blowing their whistles for us to go over the top, Billy's hand was always on my shoulder.'

'Okay Percy,' he would say. 'Keep close by me.' And he would go forward avoiding the firing line of the German machine gunners. In that way he managed to keep both of us alive long after all our comrades who'd gone to France with us in 1914 had been killed or wounded.

It was on 21 July (the battle of the Somme began on 1 July 1916) that Billy Atkins was killed at a place known as High Wood. Our battalion, or those that were left of it, had been held up by densely laid low-level barbed wire and devastating machine-gun and rifle fire. We had found some cover in a shell hole but a German machine-gunner had spotted us and kept us pinned down. The machine-gun nest was about 100 yards away (91.5m); we lay in the mud at the bottom of the shell hole waiting for a signal as to what we were to do next, but none came. We didn't know then that there was nobody left alive in our section to give an order: all the officers and NCOs were either dead or wounded. Then Billy quite suddenly said: 'This is where we part company, Percy. But don't you worry, just keep out of the line of fire of the machine guns – once they have you in their sights, you can't escape them, but riflemen have a much more difficult job to hit a moving target. Now I'm going to have a go at that machine gun.' And with that he leaped out of the shell hole and dashed for the machine gun that had us pinned down. It had remained silent for a minute or two, but now it opened up and sounded like some old woman trying to talk through her false teeth on a freezing cold morning. Bullets began to cut slices of earth off the top of the shell hole until it appeared, from where I was crouching, to rise like a brown halo above. Out into that stream of death ran my mate Billy, and as he ran towards the German lines he was literally cut to pieces by a stream of bullets. His body fell not 50 yards in front of me (46.7m) but I was charging up behind him, and as he fell the machine gun's mechanism must have stuck because it stopped firing. Then, before the Huns could get it working again, I was among them, although I can't remember how I managed it, but when my temper cooled down and I sort of came to, all four of the Germans in the machine-gun post were dead, and I was alone.

I can remember now quite vividly that I looked back along the machine-gunner's line of fire and saw it was Billy's body that had saved me, because the gunner had had to lower the angle of his sights to such a degree that it had become impossible for him to get the machine gun depressed enough for him to fire it with any accuracy, and it was possibly the effect of this that had caused the damned thing to jam.

Billy's body lay in those sights, and it was then among the silent dead, the moaning and the screaming of the dying, the whining and exploding of shells, and the rat-a-tat of machine guns

Old Percy in D Company, 1st Battalion Queens Own Royal West Kent Regiment, France 1916. (Author's collection)

and the cracking of rifles, that I noticed Billy was holding a piece of paper in his hand. It was far too dangerous for me to stay in the German machine-gun nest, so I ran back the way I had come and pulled the piece of paper from Billy's hand, and I ran on and jumped back into the shell hole from which I had followed Billy what must have been only minutes before but now seemed to have been hours ago. It was only then that I noticed blood was trickling down the fingers of my right hand and I had a searing pain up my arm. My hand was useless – a bullet had gone clean through the back and out through the palm, but I still held Billy's piece of paper; it was sticking to the blood on my fingers. I put it into my pocket before taking a bandage out of my first aid kit and lashing it round my hand. Then I waited in the shell hole till it got dark and made my way back towards our lines. As I got close I heard rifle bolts clicking into the firing position, so I started cursing those stupid bastards who were getting ready to shoot me. They told me when I got into their trench that it was only my obscene language that had saved me from being shot.

Back in our lines, I was ordered to make my way to an advanced dressing station, where a young nurse cleaned and bandaged my hand. I'd lost a lot of blood and must have passed out. I don't really know what happened after that. I woke up a couple of days later in a field hospital. I'd been stripped of my field uniform, washed, and was lying in a clean army blanket. When I came to, a doctor came to my bed. He apologised to me for reading 'my letter' that had been taken from my pocket when they had stripped me of my clothes. He said he was very sorry for what had happened with my wife, and passed Billy's piece of paper to me. I read it:

Dear Billy Atkins,

I thought I'd let you know your wife's been having an affair with some bloke, an Arthur Dennis.

Yours truly,

'It doesn't say who had written the letter?' I asked Old Percy.

'No,' he replied. 'That was all of it.'

'Who then was Arthur Dennis?' I said.

'Oh! He was Billy's "friend", the bloke who took him to the recruiting sergeant to sign on, and who was paid 3d for his trouble.'

'What happened after that?' I asked him.

After I'd read the letter the doctor said he was having me transferred back to Britain as soon as possible. I never told him the letter wasn't mine. The next day I was taken to a cross-Channel ferry and shipped back to a hospital in Southampton. The doctors there operated on my hand, but there wasn't much they could do with it. They kept me in bed for a couple of days, giving me beer to help my body replace the blood I'd lost. But while I was in bed I kept reading Billy's letter, brooding over that bastard Arthur Dennis, and formulating a plan of retribution on him and revenge on Billy's widow, because it was quite plain to me that Billy had really committed suicide – now I knew why – and those who were responsible were going to pay for it.

I was kept in the hospital for two days then given forty-eight hours' compassionate leave. That was the army's way of getting rid of men who needed to sort out personal family problems, and at the same time to make room for other wounded men who were coming into the hospital in a constant stream. But I didn't go home; I went to Maidstone instead, where I hired a set of worn civilian togs, shoes and gloves from a second-hand clothes dealer (the gloves were necessary to hide the bandage on my hand) and left my army uniform in his keeping. I then went into a couple of pubs to enquire as to the whereabouts of Arthur Dennis. He was well known round Maidstone so it didn't take me long to find him. He was doing his rounds of the pubs, on the look out for 'cannon fodder' with which to ingratiate himself to his mate, the local recruiting sergeant. The sergeant had been provided with a nice office by the War Ministry, in Maidstone's town centre, in easy reach of most of the public houses.

With the war devouring men faster than volunteers could be recruited, Arthur Dennis was having a field day in the local pubs. It had become a good business, getting patriotic men drunk then signed up to join the death machine in the trenches of northern France. I had the advantage over Dennis, though, for while he was out hunting for men (or boys) to entice into joining up, he didn't know that someone was out hunting for him. He didn't know who I was or anything about me, but I knew about him and his sordid trade, and he was for the chop. I'd seen thousands of good men die like dogs, whilst scum like him still walked the streets of Britain – but in his case not for much longer.

It was in the Seven Greys public house where I was told Arthur Dennis was most likely to be, that was the first time I set eyes on him. He was sitting on a stool in the public bar, slowly sipping at a glass of Scotch whisky, when I walked up to the pub counter and ordered a pint of beer. It was a Tuesday, market day, just like today. There were hundreds of people jostling about

– among them many young, illiterate, penniless, country bucks, as strong as oxen and as fit as fiddles, ideal for the battlefields, just the material that Arthur Dennis was looking for. It was my intention he would take me to be one of them, and it seemed he had fallen for the bait.

'Give my old mate a pint on me, landlord,' he said, and winked at the publican. It was a motion of his eye that I noticed in the mirror behind the bar.

'Thanks pal,' I said. 'That's kind of you.'

'I just thought I'd like to have someone to drink with,' replied Dennis. 'Because I've decided to join up today to fight for my king and country. Give the Hun a bloody nose, that's what I say. I'm raring to go to France and meet them Mademoiselles of Amenities the army lads are always singing about. They must be having a lot of fun over there, what with the cheap wine, fags and willing women. Are you sure that you wouldn't like to enlist, too?' He winked again at the publican, who turned away. He'd obviously heard all that verbal garbage before.

'No, not me mate,' I said. 'I'm not into that fighting lark, but I'll join you in a pint. Have this next one on me.'

We stayed in the Seven Greys for several hours, and I discovered Dennis could sure sink pints of beer with whisky chasers. But for the past couple of years I'd been drinking army rum in the trenches, and I'd discovered if the Germans didn't kill you, in the longer term the rum bloody well would. Once anyone became addicted to the stuff he became an alcoholic or apparently immune to intoxication, or both. That was, of course, until either the Germans killed him or he died of cirrhosis of the liver, or both. But I began to get fed up with plying him with beer, so I ordered pints of barley wine instead; that did the trick. He finally got into such a state he had a job to stand. Then I said to him:

'Come on old pal. We'd better go and sign up for the army. Go over to France and give those Jerries a good drubbing. Do you know the way to the recruiting office?'

'Sure I do,' he slurred. 'I'd know the way blindfolded. Come on, I'll lead the way.' And he gave a last wink to the publican through a half-closed eye, put an arm round my neck, and we lurched out through the pub door and began to sing: '*We're going to pack up our troubles in our old kit bags and smile-smile-smile.*'

But I was thinking, '*You scum bastard, I'll give you smile-smile-smile. I'm just about to knock that smile right off your ugly face. By the time me and the Germans have finished with you, you won't have anything left to smile about – nothing at all.*'

When we arrived at the recruiting office, Dennis' mate, the recruiting sergeant, was just about to shut up shop for the day. His eyes opened wide when he saw us and a big toothy smile creased his fat face. 'What have we got 'ere then?' he said.

'My mate 'ere wants to join the army,' Dennis slurred. 'Fight for king and country.'

'He looks to be a nice one, Arthur. He's got the bearing of a real soldier, too. A fine physique the lad's got. Come along with me sonny boy, and I'll take yo'r pa'tickerlers,' and he ushered me into the recruiting office with his hand pushing into the small of my back. Dennis followed him.

I pointed at Dennis. 'Him first,' I countered.

'I don't want to join up,' Dennis retorted.

'I only agreed to join up if you did, old pal,' I said. 'And you agreed.'

'I did?' he said in dazed surprise.

The sergeant began to get agitated. 'Get hold of that pen and sign your name, or put your cross, or I'll get the police down here to run the pair of you in as being drunk and disorderly,' he yelled out.

Dennis did one of his now-famous winking tricks at the sergeant, through a half-closed eyelid. 'Right then, where's the pen?' Then he began to fumble about with the 'signing up' form. I stood by and watched. No one could have made head nor tale of what Dennis scribbled on that form.

'That's no good,' I told the sergeant. 'You had better fill in the form and then get him to sign it. I'm your witness.'

'But I don't really want to join the army, I was only pretending,' Dennis said through a bout of hiccoughing. 'People get killed over there.' He held out an arm, which circled the room in an arc, but was no doubt meant to indicate the general direction of France.

'You can only die once,' I said.

'Yer, only once,' the sergeant repeated, and laughed.

Dennis was babbling incoherently by this time, as the sergeant guided his hand to sign his name.

'It's good of you to take so much trouble with him,' I told the sergeant. 'What are friends for if it's not to help one another when they're in need?'

'Those are my sentiments exactly,' replied the sergeant.

'Of course,' I said. 'I do suppose recruiting has fallen off a bit lately?'

'Yes, and the rumour is this office is to be shut up if I can't maintain my previous recruiting figures. Then I'll be sent to join my regiment in France.'

'You don't fancy that, then?'

'Not damn likely, I don't. I've seen the casualty figures. Anyway, I'm too old to go fighting now. That's a young man's game, young blokes like you; you're just the kiddies for it. Right lad, sign here.'

I picked up the pen, wrote in Billy's address and signed my name as Billy Atkins. Then, half dragging Arthur Dennis out into the street, I said to him, 'Right my old mate. Now tell me about your love affair with Mrs Dolly Atkins.'

Arthur Dennis burst into tears and started to mumble almost incoherently, 'She won't have anything to do with me, mate, she won't. When I went round to see her a couple of weeks ago, after I'd heard Billy'd been killed. She told me to clear off. She yelled at me that I'd sold Billy to the army. She hates me. I'm glad I wrote and told him I was knocking about with his wife. I bet he didn't like that.'

'I thought he was a mate of yours?' I said.

'I always hated that sanctimonious, self-righteous, Bible-bashing bastard. Now he's dead, good riddance to him, I say. He always thought he was a cut above the rest of us. He was always trying to belittle me when we were at school. He made out he could do anything and everything better that I could, but I got him into the army and got him killed – I'd laugh in his face if he was here now.'

I couldn't restrain myself any longer, and I let fly at that scumbag with my only good fist. I'd lost my temper and almost made the mistake of finishing him off there and then. But a copper came round the street corner and as soon as I saw him I pretended to be helping Arthur Dennis to his feet.

'What's going on here then?' said the policemen.

'He's fallen over, constable,' I told him. 'We've just signed on to join the army and had a few pints of beer to celebrate.'

'Get up on yer feet, and get on yer way, or I'll run the pair of you in for being drunk and disorderly in a public place,' he said. 'Come on now, on yer way.'

That policemen never knew how close he was to finding Arthur Dennis's dead body when he turned round that corner, but I did as the constable had ordered: pulled Arthur Dennis up and put my arm round his shoulder, staggered down the road until we turned the corner into the next street, and I let him fall on to the footpath. I then went to the second-hand clothes dealer's shop, changed back into my army uniform, and made my way to the railway station, where I caught a train from Maidstone to London, and then from London on to Southampton.

When I got back to the hospital in Southampton, no one asked me how I'd fared. It was accepted that I'd gone to sort out a family problem. The authorities thought I'd gone home; they never even enquired of me whether I was married. Not one of them to this day has ever found out that I wasn't married at that time. They must have been under the impression it was my wife that had 'gone off the rails', as the saying goes, and they had enough on their plate dealing with the wounded and the dying to concern themselves with the trivial problems of the walking wounded.

'Well, what happened after that?' I asked him.

When I arrived back at the hospital in Southampton, I'd felt better at discovering Billy's widow was not involved with that death-dealing bastard, Arthur Dennis, and it made me more resolute than ever to put my plan for dealing with that parasite into operation. I hung about the hospital for a couple of weeks as my hand had to be dressed twice a day, and it had become obvious to me that it was never going to be of any use to me, other than to fill the fingers of a glove. Then, having been seen by the army surgeon, he told me my war service was over and I would not be returned to my regiment in France; any other man in the trenches of Flanders, the Somme or Passchendaele, facing those German rifles, machine guns and howitzers, would have jumped over the moon for joy. But the surgeon's decision made the next stage of my plan difficult, because I had to get back to France.

I had written to one of my mates with the 1st West Kents, a bloke called Tom Black, who worked in the cookhouse. I knew there was a good chance he'd still be alive. I asked him to let me know when the next draft of volunteers was to be brought up to the line, as I had an old friend who'd joined the regiment and just included the initials A.D. The censors were not too strict on letters going to men in the line. He was a shrewd character who'd wangled the cookhouse job to avoid being in the trenches; he knew the score with the censors, and wrote:

Dear Percy, old mate,

I got the letter you sent. I'm glad to hear you are comfortable at the Military Hospital in Southampton.

I expect you'll be back here with us soon, when you come bring us some Kent apples, the last lot you sent arrived last week, most of them have already gone. In the meantime be good, see you soon,

Your old mates

Tom and Arthur D.

It was about five days before I'd received the letter from Tom that Arthur Dennis had arrived at a reception centre with 324 other recruits: the date was 17 August 1916. Those men and boys were to fill some of the battalion losses of the first few weeks of the Battle of the Somme. I knew there was no time to waste, so I changed out of my hospital uniform into my battle dress and made my way to the harbour to catch a ferry bound for France. I had retained the leather gloves I'd got in Maidstone and had pulled them over my bandaged hand to hide it, but on several occasions I was stopped by Redcaps and asked for my army pay book. It was quite easy to fool them, I found, by simply asking them to retrieve the pay book from my pocket and I would show them my hand, or perhaps they would never believe that anyone in their right mind would be stupid enough to try getting back to the front line. Whatever the case was, they let me pass without too much hindrance once they had seen my bandaged hand and explained I'd been to England to have it operated on, and was now returning to my battalion. It was always: 'Right mate, on your way,' with a wave of the thumb.

When I got back to the battalion it was in billets at Metigny. It had been almost reformed after its losses on the Somme. It had gone into the battle with close to 1,100 officers and other ranks. It came out to rest and reform with less than 350.

'All those men,' I wondered.

'That wasn't unusual,' he said. 'Most of the chum regiments had suffered worse casualties: some of them had been wiped out altogether on the first day of the battle, and by the time I'd been wounded and Billy Atkins had been killed thousands more men and boys had been poured into the battle and liquidated.'

'All those men in a few days,' I repeated.

Yes, and that's what I said to the sergeant major after he'd told me. It's worse than the losses we had in the battle on Hill 60. But I have to admit, the sergeant major was actually pleased to see me, or at least he appeared to be. I had only been away a month, but almost every man I met was a new face to me. Man, I say – it would be closer to the truth to say 'every boy', because they all looked like a lot of wide-eyed schoolboys. It didn't occur to me at that time I'd been in France almost two years – I was nineteen years of age – and I was still alive. However, at that moment I only had one interest, only one thought playing on my mind and that was to find Arthur Dennis.

At first the sergeant major wanted to put me on some light duties, but I insisted I wanted to go back into my old company, D Company.

'Without your mate, Billy Atkins?' he said.

'Yes,' I said. 'Because his friend Arthur Dennis has joined the battalion. Now, if you could arrange to have him seconded to D Company where I can keep an eye on him, I'd be very much obliged.'

'He is in D Company,' he retorted. 'And by the way, Brooks, the battalion has taken a hell of a pounding as you can see by the number of replacements, and you're not included to be one of them. I don't know what you're doing back here, and I'm damn sure you shouldn't be, but I need you son. None of these new lads have seen any fighting, so you'll be the senior private in D Company now. You just make sure they keep a steady nerve in the line during their first few days in the trenches.'

'Okay, sergeant major,' I replied, and left him to join D Company just as they were moving out of the rest area to march up to the line.

I quickly found Arthur Dennis. He was a great avoider. He almost always managed to avoid guards, trench digging and trench repairing, laying or repairing the barbed wire entanglements in front of our trenches. He managed to avoid almost everything, except me.

When I saw him I remembered him right away, but he never recognised me as being his drinking partner in the Seven Greys pub in Maidstone, and the bloke responsible for his being in the army right then. But I avoided mixing with or even talking to him. When he was out of earshot of the sergeants or officers, he was always bleating to anyone who'd listen that he'd been brought into the army by mistake. He even got the military authorities to clarify that it was his signature on the signing up form with the recruiting sergeant, but unfortunately for him the recruiting sergeant had confirmed he had signed up with his friend, Billy Atkins. It was unfortunate too, that Billy Atkins could not be found. The Maidstone police, accompanied by Military Police, had gone to Billy's house to arrest him, but were shocked to find that he had been killed in action during the battle of the Somme, and they therefore assumed it was someone else that had signed up with Arthur Dennis and had given a false name and address on the recruitment form – they were unable to trace that miscreant.

When Arthur Dennis was told this information, he became silent and withdrawn, and as one young Kentish country bumpkin remarked without knowing the facts: 'It's as though Arthur's being shadowed by a ghost.'

'What happened then?' I asked.

The sergeant major had come to me and told me what had happened. 'Keep an eye on that Arthur Dennis, Brooks,' he ordered. 'It seems he has complained he enlisted with some bloke who has failed to report for service. I don't know all the details but the Military Police have not been able to trace the other fellow yet. You have to keep a special eye open on men who associate with that type of individual.'

'What type of individual is that, sergeant major?' I asked him.

'You know what I mean, Brooks, cowards. Damn cowards,' he replied.

But whether he was a coward or not, Arthur Dennis was in the line: the front line where death was your shadow even without being in the light of the sun. He was now where he'd placed my mate, Billy Atkins. In the morning we would be going over the top to attack the German front line. Arthur Dennis was about to face what Billy Atkins had faced dozens of times before he died: death. It was going to be interesting watching to see if he had the same resolution and courage as my dead friend, but from what I'd already seen of him, I very much doubted it.

The order for us to go over the top was set for 0700 after a heavy artillery barrage that was supposed to soften up enemy resistance, although I'd never noticed it having that effect in the past – the Germans were always ready and waiting for us. But at 0700 the whistles began to shrill out all along the line, and as we began to clamber over the parapets out of our trenches, on to the newly created moonscape of shell craters, across the remnants of barbed-wire entanglements, it was then the Jerry machine guns began to chatter merrily away. By comparison, the Charge of the Light Brigade in the Crimean War was like a game of cowboys and Indians, as into those whispering, whistling bullets calmly strode the descendants of the Dirty Half Hundred, the 50th of Foot, the Queen's Own RWKR.

For my part in that bloody catastrophe, I followed Arthur Dennis as I'd followed Billy Atkins – very closely – but for a different reason. I was waiting for the inevitable German wall of rifle fire and stick grenades, when we got within a few dozen yards of their forward trenches, that would scythe our lads down by the dozen, and along the whole line by the hundreds and thousands. Arthur Dennis, as I had anticipated, dove into the nearest shell hole he came to, like a rabbit going to earth; I followed him. The advance on our section of the line quickly petered out, as the German machine-gunners and riflemen almost obliterated the whole of our company. Our lads lay in a carpet of dead and dying, between the German trenches and ours. I must admit it wasn't as bad as the first day's battle of the Somme. There were a few of us left after this catastrophic cock-up, but not many. Arthur Dennis, on the other hand, was lying near the top of a shell hole, whimpering.

'Come on Dennis, out you go,' I said to him.

He turned round and his face showed both surprise and recognition: 'It's you, you bastard. The bloke who got me to sign myself into this hell on earth,' he raved.

'That's right,' I told him. 'And here's the reason why …' And I thrust the letter he'd written to Billy Atkins into his shaking hands. He looked down at the letter in disbelief.

'So that's it. You've brought me out here because of that,' and he threw the letter down into the shell hole.

'Yes, that's it. You are responsible for the death of my mate, Billy Atkins. You got the Germans to do your dirty work for you, but it was you, your letter, that was the cause of his death. You thought you were clever and would get away with it, but now it's your turn. I'm going to give you one chance though, by giving you some advice. The way I saw it as I jumped into this shell hole after you was: there's a machine-gun nest about 25 yards away (23m) directly in front of us and behind their barbed wire. If you can cover that ground and knock that machine gun out, you'll be free to take your chances with the army till the end of the war; and if you don't have a go at it I'm going to shoot you here and now. That's your choice, so are you ready, now over the top you go.'

I prodded him with my bayonet, but he just stared at me in total disbelief. 'You're mad, bloody mad,' he yelled, but both fear and hatred showed in his eyes.

'Get out, you bastard,' I repeated, so he turned round and leaped out of the shell hole. He didn't even bother to take a look out over the rim of the shell hole before he made off; he just went. When I peered over the rim, I saw him standing in the machine-gun nest, alone.

There wasn't a German to be seen. Then he jumped behind the machine gun yelling, 'It's your turn now.'

But before he could pull the trigger, a shell from our own side landed on top of him and he was blown to smithereens. Justice, in my eyes, had not only been done, it had been seen to be done; now I had to get back to my own lines, alive. I knew from long experience that if I tried to get back during daylight, a sniper was sure to get me. So I lay in the shell hole until it got dark, not wishing to draw fire from a sniper or another machine-gunner further down the German trench system. Then I crawled slowly back through that rat-infested, open-air mortuary among the dead, no-man's-land, towards the British lines. The remnants of the 1st West Kents had been pulled out of the line to reform, after the terrible losses in men it had suffered. As I got close to our trenches, I heard the rifle bolts clicking back into the firing position, and began swearing at those stupid bastards in the forward trench for all I was worth, and it was just my bad luck that they were men of the Scottish Border Regiment, most of whom only spoke some form of Gaelic. A couple of them grabbed me as I crawled into their trench. They would have beaten me to death if their officer hadn't quickly turned up, recognised my khaki uniform, and told them to belay their activities – at least till he had established my identity. Once it had been established who I was, I was sent back behind the lines to the reserve area. There was pandemonium going on as more young men, straight from training camps in England, were being formed into platoons and companies, ready to reinforce the Scottish Border Regiment holding that section of the line.

When I got back to my section, the sergeant major grabbed me. 'Where the hell have you been?' he said. 'There's been all sorts of problems over you. You have been reported as being absent without leave by the Southampton Military Hospital. The commanding officer has received a letter to that effect, but I told him you were back with the battalion. I thought you'd bought it today with most of the rest of the lads, but now you're back here. We'd better go and see him.'

I was promptly marched over to a tent, which was serving as the CO's office. 'Private Brooks 9072, sir,' said the sergeant major. 'Reported as being absent without leave by Southampton Military Hospital, sir.'

The CO looked up from the never-ending casualty lists he was perusing, then in a tired voice said, 'What have you to say for yourself, Brooks? You've heard the charge, are you in fact a deserter?'

'No,' I replied. 'I can't be a deserter because I'm back with my battalion, sir.'

'If I may be permitted to speak, sir,' interjected the sergeant major. 'Brooks has just returned from the line.'

'The line, SM? Do you mean the front line?'

'Yes, sir, he was with D Company when they attacked the German trenches this morning. He's one of only a dozen of our men that made it back to our lines.'

'Oh. Really? Were you aware Brooks had returned to the battalion and had gone into the trenches with them?'

'Yes sir, I did know,' was the sergeant major's reply. 'The quick answer, as I see it sir, is that Brooks is not absent without leave, because he is back with his battalion where he belongs. On the other hand, I have to concede he is absent from the Military Hospital in Southampton where he is supposed to be. I suggest you order Brooks to return to the Military Hospital, with a letter explaining where he's been, and let them deal with him. The information we have on Brooks from the hospital is that his hand is so badly damaged he will never again be fit for military service, sir.'

'I see,' said the CO. 'Right Brooks. You shall return to the Military Hospital in Southampton. You will do as you're damn well told by the hospital authorities. You shall not return to France unless you are officially ordered to return to the battalion. What you did by returning here reflects on the discipline of my battalion, and our regiment. If there should be a repetition of this act in the future, you shall be dealt with most severely. In fact, I should be recommending you go before a court martial, where if you were found guilty of desertion, you would be shot. Do I make myself clear?'

'Yes, sir,' I replied. They were the only two words I was allowed to speak during the whole of that interview.

'That's all, Brooks,' the CO said. 'The SM will give you your order. You are dismissed.'

''Shun,' barked the sergeant major. 'About turn. By the left quick march.' And we left the tent with the CO at his desk, sorting out his casualty figures, and writing letters of condolences to the next of kin of his lost battalion.

When we were outside the CO's office, the sergeant major looked me up and down in the same way as he had all the men when we were on inspection parades. At first I thought he was going to tell me to 'get your bloody hair cut' – that was his usual starting point when he intended to have a go at you – but then he said in what I thought was a fatherly way: 'I don't know why you came back here, Brooks. You no doubt had your own reasons. But only a madman would have come back knowing what is happening here. Not like that coward Arthur Dennis, although he must have bought it because he never returned from our last attack on the German lines. Now I'm sending you back to Southampton Military Hospital with a letter explaining you had a lapse of memory, and when you get there, stay there until you get your discharge papers from the army on medical grounds. Then you may survive this damn crazy war, right?'

'Sure sergeant,' I replied.

'By the way, Brooks,' he said. 'I'm pleased you did come back. I doubt if we shall ever meet again, good luck.' And he held his hand out and we shook hands – that was the last I ever saw of him.

'Thanks sergeant,' I said. 'And may I say good luck to you, too.'

Old Percy went silent for a while until I brought him back to life with: 'Well, what happened then?'

Do you mean to the sergeant major? He was killed the following day when the battalion went back into the line in support of the King's Own Scottish Border Regiment. I reported back to Southampton Military Hospital, where the doctors weren't too happy when they saw the state of my wounded hand after my escapade in the trenches, but they sorted it out to the best of their ability. In the meantime, some of we wounded were allowed out to various functions that were laid on by sports clubs and other voluntary organisations. One place we were invited to was just outside Southampton; it was a bowls club by the name of the Waverley Club. The people there were very kind to us. They obviously knew we had been wounded but they had not the slightest idea what was going on just across the English Channel.

He stopped talking and I had to prompt him again: 'Go on,' I said:

Well, after a further few weeks of treatment to my hand. I was sent to Ireland and attached to a labour battalion based in Dublin. As you know, there was a lot of trouble going on after the Easter Rebellion of 1916. We wounded men were used to help the police flush out men that we called terrorists, and the Irish call patriots. This went on till 1919 when I was returned back to England to be demobilised. I was stationed in a barracks at Chelmsford, Essex. That's where I met and married your mother. That was the story until today when I came here to Maidstone to see Billy Atkins' widow. I had a feeling that if she was still alive she would visit this place today. I knew she and Billy always came here on 21 July, because he had told me they did. It was odds on that if she was still alive she would come here today. She is a nice lady, isn't she? No wonder Billy loved her so much – too much, it cost him his life, although I doubt if he would have survived the war in the trenches.

'Well,' I said. 'What a story. That Arthur Dennis had a lot to answer for.'

'Yes,' replied Old Percy. 'Because he wasn't only responsible for causing Billy's death, but he sentenced his lovely wife to servitude for the rest of her life. I don't think the death sentence was too harsh a penalty, do you?'

'Come on,' I said. 'That was a long time ago, let's go home.'

We got up out of the seat, walked slowly back along the towpath, past the fishermen and the swans and ducks; past the boathouse on the opposite shore, out through the cast-iron gates into the market place where stallholders were still hawking their wares. Some places don't ever seem to change much when I come to think about it, nor do people, do they? But what a terrible price some of our people have had to pay for it.

Postscript

When Old Percy died a year or two after our visit to Maidstone market, and his body had been cremated, I should have taken his ashes to France and scattered them where most of his young comrades lay buried, on Hill 60 or near the banks of the rivers Aisne or Somme. That's where I'm sure he would have found the peace of mind he'd always sought, but had never found among the living after the trauma of his youthful escapades. I'm quite sure too, he would have rested far more easily among the souls of his young comrades on the battlefields of France, with the lost battalions of the king's armies, than in the garden of the local crematorium.

Facts as to the Overall Cost of the First World War

In his report to the Carnegie Foundation (1934), Dr Nicholas Murray–Butler stated that the financial cost of the war was estimated to have been £80,000 million. This sum, according to Dr Murray–Butler, would have been sufficient to buy up the whole of France and Belgium and everything they contained five times over.

The cost in human life in round figures was calculated as being:

Killed outright: 10 million. Severely wounded: 6,300,000. Slightly wounded: 14 million, which did not include those ex-servicemen and civilians who were traumatised by their wartime experiences, or later died of their wounds or from disease. Then in the influenza epidemic that followed, said to have been a direct consequence of the war, a further 10 million people died.

However the Allied politicians declared it to have been a Great and Glorious Victory. But for whom?

TALE 5

OUR ERNIE A FALLEN HERO! A MUTINEER? WHAT A DAMN CHEEK!

I had known Ernie Smith, or I thought I'd known him, all my life. Now here he was, my workmate in a Thames lighter, stripped down to his waist with sweat running out of every visible pore of his body, as he strained every sinew in his muscles, running back and forth between the slowly rising piles of pig-lead ingots that were being discharged from a John Ellerman line cargo ship at 24 transit shed, Tilbury Docks, working as hard as any Trojan warrior ever had. But I was soon to learn something about Ernie that I'd never known before this encounter with him.

Ernie was older than me by some six years, but he and his family had lived on the same council housing estate as had mine. Of course, he had known my elder brothers and sisters, they all being in the same age group as he, and they had all attended the same schools in Gravesend, Kent.

I, on the other hand, being several years younger, only knew Ernie by sight before entering the port transport industry. That is, of course, with the exception of a few months' period at the beginning of the Second World War, when many of we children from Gravesend were evacuated to Norfolk on 3 September 1939, by Thames pleasure steamers. However, Ernie wasn't evacuated for very long. He was returned home to Gravesend as soon as he reached his fourteenth birthday, so that he could start work (bombs or no bombs), for that was the lot of working-class children in those days.

It was a hot July afternoon, really hot, with the sun high in the heaven, and small white wisps of clouds scattered across a light blue, heat-hazed sky. It was so hot, in fact, that even the raucously noisy, ever-hungry seagulls had deserted us (at mobile time, too, when they generally benefited from the odd crusts of bread and stale sandwiches the dockers and Lightermen threw down for them) and had gone off to the riverside to paddle in the mud of the foreshore, or for a dip in the cool but polluted, stinking waters of the River Thames.

The mobile tea van had turned up and parked on the shaded side of 26 transit shed. The top-hands had called out 'beer-ho', and we dockers had come off the ship and out of the Thames lighters. Then, when we had finished drinking our tea and eaten our chunks of cake or bread pudding, and the PLA-embossed tea mugs had been returned to the mobile tea van, Jesse, the Port of London Authority 'mobile van tea lady' who had been serving us, closed the

Ernie Smith in Royal Navy uniform after being called up for military service. (By kind permission of Mrs Smith)

hatch of the mobile and drove off along the quay laughing, after telling us how lucky *we* were to be able to strip down to the waist 'in this weather', and not to have to be encumbered with a bra and other things, only to be told laughingly by one of the dockers: 'I'm sure we don't know what you're talking about, Jesse. We wouldn't object if you stripped down to your waist, removed your bra, your "encumbrances" and your other things, whatever they may be. Would we lads?'

Of course, he got an earful of verbal invectives from Jesse that brought bouts of laughter from the assembled dockers and Lightermen. Then Jesse, acting as haughtily as any of the madames parading down a Parisian boulevard, had turned her nose up in the air, and being a woman, making sure she was going to have the last word called out as she drove off along the dock quayside: 'Back to work you peasants, I'll see you in the morning – that's if you're not all melted away by then, ha-ha-ha.' And with a wave of her hand out of the van window, she was gone. (Thank God for the good humour of the mobile canteen tea ladies.)

The ship's hatch we were working out of was discharging half-hundred-weight ingots of pig-lead into Thames lighters. The vessel was named the city of something or other (all the ships owned by the John Ellerman line were named after a city), and this particular vessel, which was inward-bound from South Africa, for the sake of it having a name, I shall call the *City of Durban*. There you are, I've named the ship without having to waste a bottle of vintage champagne or having to pay out for a banquet for 'hangers-on' who would, on such auspicious occasions as the launching of a brand new vessel, be invited to be wined and dined at the ship-builders' expense. However, I dare say that such generous gestures on behalf of shipbuilders usually generate publicity in the media and possibly secure the sale of a ship or two?

The *City of Durban* had been berthed, and made secure, to her moorings at number 26 transit shed, on her starboard side. This was quite simply because the ship was discharging general cargo, both ashore on to the quay by the use of cranes, and pig-lead 'over-side' into Thames lighters.

The ship's discharging gang, with whom I was working, were operating under the ship's own winches and derricks, using a 'union purchase' (that is two derricks, one plumbing the centre of the ship's hold, and one the centre of the Thames lighter). These two static steel pole contraptions carried wire cables from the winches' drums, under heel blocks bolted to the deck or a bulkhead, to the derricks' heads, where they were threaded round steel pulleys, then shackled to swivels, that held the 'union purchase' in place. The system, when it was fully rigged, was powered by two of the ship's winches.

It was mid-afternoon, by which time we had almost completed loading another lighter with 80 tons of pig-lead, our third lighter that day – just one more craft would take us up to 7p.m. and knocking-off time. Our discharging tonnage target was 320 tons plus. *Thank God*, I thought. *Only another 80 tons or more?*

I had been picked up as a 'pro-rata man' to a regular ship's gang that was discharging pig-lead out of the deep tanks in number 3 hold of the *City of Durban*.

A ship discharging a cargo of lead was considered to be a good, well-paid job in the docks. The piecework rate for discharging pig-lead was 3*s* 2*d* per ton, divided between twelve men. The pig-lead ingots weighed 56lb each (25.4kg) or 40 ingots to the ton. It was an easy, clean job by docking standards. That is unless you managed to crush a finger or two. We had almost completed the loading of a Thames lighter, having placed the pig-lead in regular piles of forty ingots, five piles wide across the width of the craft, and sixteen piles along its length, that were kept uniform running from stem to stern for the full length of the craft.

We had just finished stowing a set of pig-lead when the crack of the union purchase above our heads heralded the arrival of another set. Ernie looked up towards the ship's bulwark then he muttered in surprise, 'Christ! That's Benson.'

When I looked up I saw a tallish, broad-shouldered, dark haired, ordinary-looking OST clerk, holding a tally pad and pencil, trying to check the number of ingots in the piles of pig-lead that we had already stowed in the lighter.

'Who is he, then?' I said, not understanding the relevance of Ernie's surprise.

'Benson? Bloody hell, mate,' he said. 'That man is part of a legend. He's ex-Special Air Service.'

'What!' I replied in surprise. 'That bloke up there, he doesn't look as though he could upend a nutmeg.'

'No he doesn't, does he?' said Ernie. 'But the last time I saw him, our airborne battalion were going out to make a raid in France. The Dakota we were in had a separate door in the rear of the aircraft. Before we got to our target, the red "prepare to jump" light went on and six men armed to the teeth with every weapon you can think of came out of the rear cabin. Not one of them said a word to any of us – they stood by the exit door and waited for the green light to flash on – and left the Dakota on a separate mission of their own; Benson was one of them. To look at him you wouldn't think he could harm a fly – but I wouldn't want to be on the receiving end of an argument with him.'

We finished loading the lighter; Benson climbed down the ship's side rope ladder into the lighter; he checked the number of pig-lead ingots in the separated stacks athwart and fore and aft of the craft; then he climbed back up the rope ladder on to the ship's deck. He never even looked at Ernie or me, nor did he speak. It was as though we didn't exist.

'Are we invisible?' I asked Ernie. 'I don't think he saw us working here.'

'He saw us all right,' Ernie replied. 'Blokes like him don't miss much; they don't talk much, either.' That was that.

On our having completed the loading of the lighter, the top-hand then called for a Lighterman to float the loaded craft out, and to bring an empty craft back under number three hatch's derricks. A rope was thrown down from the ship's deck which the Lighterman attached to an after bollard of the craft; the capstan on the ship's after-deck began to slowly revolve; the heavily laden lighter scraped along the ship's side and moved out under the stern of the ship; the rope attached to the capstan from the lighter's after bollard was removed; and the lighter was then steered to the quayside to await a tug to pull it out of the docks through the lock gates into the river, before towing it on to its destination at some wharf or other, further up the river.

In the meantime, Ernie and I made our way up the ship's side rope ladder to the deck, where we turned on the deck water hose and washed away the sweat that was running down our faces and bodies. Then we went to the ship's galley and scrounged some drinking water from the chef (the ship's cook) and sat down on adjacent bollards at the ship's stern, to await the arrival of our next Thames lighter. Then I opened the conversation:

'I wasn't aware you were in the airborne forces during the last war, Ernie,' I said.

Ernie sat for a full minute in silence before he answered, then he replied: 'No! Then that's something best forgotten about.'

'Why's that?' I asked him.

'Because of what happened shortly after we arrived in Malaya.'

'What was that?'

'The whole battalion was charged with mutiny.'

'Mutiny! Jesus Christ, Ernie,' I said. 'They [the army] could have had you shot for that.'

'Some of us very nearly were,' he replied. 'We were threatened with it.'

'How did that come about?' I asked him.

'Well,' he said. 'We were the 13th Parachute Battalion, 6th Airborne Division. We had been drafted out to the Far East to stand by for the American invasion of Japan. We were, at first, sent to the Isle of Java, which at that time was still a part of the Dutch East Indies. We had been placed in what was loosely described as a "rest camp". The conditions in that camp, known as the Semarang rest camp, were intolerable. They were so bad our commanding officer made representations on our behalf describing the conditions we were living in as "shocking", but worse was to come.

Ernie Smith in Airborne uniform after
being transferred into the army, 1944.
(By kind permission of Mrs Smith)

Ernie Smith in Java, Dutch East Indies,
before being charged with mutiny. (By
kind permission of Mrs Smith)

After having spent three months in the Semarang rest camp, the complaints made on our battalion's behalf about the conditions by our CO must have filtered through to someone in higher authority, because we were re-drafted to a place called Muar in Malaya, not far from Kuala Lumpur, the state capital in West Malaysia. The place was said to be another rest camp, and if it was, it was a rest camp with a difference; the conditions were even worse in Muar. In fact they could be better described as 'deplorably shocking'.

The 'rest camp' consisted of rows of saturated tents, set up in what can only be described as a swamp or quagmire. The whole area in which the rest camp had been laid out was waterlogged, and made worse by torrential monsoon rains. The floors inside the tents were ankle deep in decaying vegetation, mixed with earth to make a black, clinging constituency of stinking mud. There were no beds for the men, few washing facilities, just four taps, three to be used by the whole unit, and one was set aside for the exclusive use of sergeants. The latrines were not fit to be used by human beings; it was a deplorable place, certainly nothing the British Army should be proud to admit it subjected its fighting soldiers to, let alone to charge them with mutiny.

'So where were the officers and sergeants living?'

'I don't know where they were billeted,' he replied. 'They were certainly not sharing the luxurious lifestyle of our rest camp. But that wasn't the end of the saga as far as we troops were concerned, nor the worst part of it. Because now we come to the most important part: cooking facilities in the rest camp were almost non-existent and what food we got was diabolical, and had to be eaten sitting beside stinking culverts and open drains. At one period we were without food for two days, on another occasion we had no bread for three days. Our breakfasts, if we should have been so lucky, consisted of a ladle of porridge, a single slice of bread and a piece of bacon. For lunch, if we were lucky, we got a spoonful of sardines and a piece of cheese – cheese being the operative word in this case as we paratroopers became, as expressed in army jargon, cheesed off. Yet in these filthy, diabolical conditions, that were almost as bad as those our fathers had had to contend with on the battlefields of France during the First World War, we were expected to turn out on parade each day with our kit cleaned, brasses shining and our webbings and gaiters freshly blancoed. Those men who did not turn out impeccably dressed were punished with the greatest severity.

We had put up with these atrocious conditions for months, but by May 1946 we had had enough, so on the 14th we went on strike.'

'You silly sot,' I told him. 'You can't go on strike in the army.'

'Well,' replied Ernie. 'We called it a "strike", but the army chose to call it a "mutiny". I suppose it was the army's way of covering up the mishandling of the situation, by shoving the blame on the victims of their administration, or whatever. They soon had us surrounded by the 1st Battalion the Devonshire Regiment, with fixed bayonets. We were then bundled into lorries and driven to a compound, where more armed British troops were brought in to make sure we didn't escape.'

'So what did the Officer Corps decide to do then?' I asked him. 'After all, man for man, you paratroopers could have taken on those poor bloody infantrymen, had you a mind to.'

'Yes, but we didn't have a mind to,' he replied. 'All we wanted was to get some decent billets, where we could get dry and where we had facilities to get clean water and some decent food.

Instead, the army had us surrounded by even more companies of fully-armed infantrymen, while they had us caged up behind a thousand rolls of barbed wire. By this time the whole scenario appeared to be based on a White Hall farce, so all we paras burst into singing that war-time song:

> *Let me be by myself in the evening breeze,*
> *And listen to the murmur of the cottonwood trees,*
> *And send me off forever, but I ask you please,*
> *Don't fence me in.*

At first it was all good humoured on our part; but the Officer Corps had other ideas. It was soon obvious they intended to make an example of us, because other units in Malaya were also rebelling about the conditions they were expected to live in. So the army set up an investigation into the "mutiny", by calling in the army's Special Investigation Branch of the Royal Military Police.'

'How long did the investigation take?'

'I don't know exactly, but it was three months before we were brought before a court martial. Our defending officer was warned not to defend us too well, but he was a good bloke and advised us all to write home to our families and explain to them what was happening. We were held behind barbed wire all that time. In the meantime, we were constantly being warned by our redcap interrogators that the penalty for mutiny in wartime was death.'

'I bet that made you proud to be a British soldier, didn't it?'

'It did. We were penned up and living on field-punishment rations, which I must admit, weren't any worse than what we had been given in the rest camp. Outside our prison, we could see Japanese prisoners of war strutting about unguarded, and virtually free to do as they pleased.'

It was at this point the top-hand shouted at us: 'Come on you two mouthy sots. This isn't the bloody House of Commons. We don't get paid for sitting on our arses creating hot air. There's work to do; come on, get down into that lighter, there's a set of pig-lead waiting for you. Hurry up or we won't finish this soddin' job today.'

However, we did finish discharging the pig-lead that evening, and I, being a pro-rata man, was paid off. I never worked with Ernie Smith again after that job. One reason for that may have been because I was injured in a ship-board accident, so my days as a real working docker were ended. But I often saw Ernie about the docks and even more so when, under the permanent employment scheme that was finally introduced into the Port of London in the late 1960s, we were allocated to work for the same shipping company employer.

The port transport industry was organised and run on much the same lines as the military, with most of the higher management having been ex-officers from one of the three armed services, and the mercantile marines. Ernie was allocated to work by the National Dock Labour Board as: Smith E.J., NDLB No 3/3135602. Metropolitan Terminal Pay No. – 467.

Metropolitan Terminals Limited was the contracting ship servicing company for the West Coast of Africa Conference Lines. It was the company to which I myself was allocated on the introduction of permanent employment, and where I was employed at that time in the capacity of a ship's clerk, attached to the southern quay's offices. That was from where Ernie left the docks industry, and the next time I heard of him was at my sister's funeral, when I met Ernie's widow, Joyce.

Joyce and I sat talking for some time about the docks; about the fears and the tears of those 'dabbing days', and sometimes 'dabbing weeks'; we talked of trying to raise a family when there were no ships, no work and the only guaranteed income was the 'fall-back money' paid out to each man at the end of each week. That was provided, of course, he had attended the 'free call' eleven times during any one week, 7.45 a.m. and 12.45 p.m. Monday to Saturday, and had a full book of attendance stamps. Otherwise he received no wages at all.

We talked about how Ernie and his compatriots would tout round the local farms for a job, any job, in order to make ends meet – driving lorries, tractors or other farm implements, or picking peas, potatoes or fruit – anything to scratch a livelihood, anything. I knew just what she meant. I'd been there and done it all myself, many times, but such mundane things as the socio-economic problems it brought to dockers' families were not considered important enough for media barons to broadcast or publish. They were only interested in reporting 'work stoppages', not the cause and effect of them – similar to the attitude of politicians and officers of the British army when dealing with the welfare of its soldiers and their families.

It was during this conversation that Joyce asked me: 'Did you know Ernie and his comrades were threatened with being shot for mutiny?'

'Yes,' I replied. 'I did know that.' But I sat and listened as she continued.

'Well,' she began. 'The so-called mutiny began on 14 May 1946, when the men of the 13th Parachute Battalion refused to go on parade. The reason for refusing to parade was simply because they were being forced to live in conditions so appalling that it was said even Malayan farmers wouldn't have subjected or expected their animals to have tolerated such treatment. The paras thought they were going on strike, and that their protest would bring their predicament to the notice of the appropriate authorities. They were kept behind barbed wire until the trial began on 11 August 1946.'

'That was an interesting date for the trial to begin,' I told her. 'It was a year after the Japanese surrendered.'

'Was it really?' she said, not fully realising the significance of the date.

We spoke at some length about the 'strike' and its immediate consequences, and about the sterling work of the defending officer, a Captain J.F. Reilly. I told Joyce I would look further into the strike, so I did.

The Facts

Now it has to be accepted that the armed services do not recognise the word 'strike' (as in the context of stopping work) under King's or Queen's Regulations. The refusal of obeying a direct order by one or more men is construed to be a mutiny, so Trooper Smith E. Army No – 14990625, 13th Parachute Battalion, 6th Airborne Division, was charged with 262 of his comrades with mutiny under the King's Regulations.

Actually, Ernie Smith's story begins on 6 June 1944 (D-Day), when he was called up for military service. He travelled to Liverpool to join the Royal Navy but was transferred into the

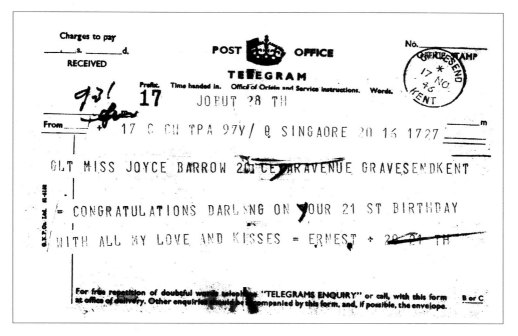

A telegram sent to Miss Joyce Barrows by Trooper Ernie Smith after his release from Changi Military Prison, Singapore. (By kind permission of Mrs Smith)

army on 19 August 1944, and joined the 2nd Battalion, the Royal East Kent Regiment, the Third Regiment of Foot, the Buffs. After his initial training, Ernie volunteered for service with the airborne forces, principally because the pay was an extra shilling each week, which he could send home to his mother. The extra dangers inherent in being a parachutist never entered his head. After intensive training, he was accepted into the 13th Parachute Battalion, 6th Airborne Division, where he continued his training in all the various war courses with particular emphasis in the use of rifle and bayonet, hand grenades, sten guns, PIATs (shoulder-held anti-tank guns), unarmed combat and the obligatory eight parachute jumps, before he was awarded his Red Devils beret, the coveted wings and badge of the airborne divisions, which he received on 22 January 1945. Then, on 27 January 1945, he had fourteen days embarkation leave before being sent on by troopship to Java, to prepare for the American invasion of Japan – an invasion that never materialised because two atom bombs were exploded over Japan, at Nagasaki and Hiroshima. These ultimate acts of aggression by America were a final humiliation on the Japanese people and empire. The atom bombs brought death and destruction on an unprecedented scale to a civilian population and precipitated a quick end to the Pacific War.

The so called 'Malayan Mutiny' by men of the 13th Battalion, 6th Airborne Division, was said to have begun when 262 battle-hardened veterans, many of whom had taken part in the D-Day air assault on German defences behind the lines, before the British and Canadian sea assault on Gold, Sword and Juno beaches of the Normandy coast had begun, were charged with mutiny for failing to 'fall in' for morning parade on 14 May 1946.

Their reason:

> The intolerable living conditions they were being forced to experience, due to either the lack
> of ability on the part of senior officers to remedy the situation, or a total disregard by senior
> officers to safeguard the welfare of their men.

From all the evidence at hand, it would appear there was a dereliction of duty by those
officers, whose duty and responsibility it was to make adequate provisions for the benefit of,
and reasonable comfort of, their trained fighting troops. More especially as there was every
possibility the troops would need to be fully fit, should they have been required for the invasion
of the Japanese mainland.

However it has to be pointed out, this was not the first occasion on which soldiers in the
Far East had gone 'on strike'. For when a Major-General Arkwright took the stand before the
court martial, he openly admitted the paratroopers' camp was 'not what it might be'. The court
was left in no doubt that all over the Far East there were camps that were degrading to the
men. He made no direct mention, however, that other servicemen had demonstrated outside
the headquarters of the Allied Land Services, South East Asia Command, against the appalling
living conditions at the notorious Changi camp, and that no punishment had been levied
against them. Why was that, one has to ask oneself.

In the case of the mutiny by 13th Parachute Battalion, 6th Airborne Division, it is recorded
that no high-ranking officer had seen fit to discover why such highly trained, battle-hardened
veterans had acted out of character. The court martial that was chosen to try the paratroopers
was presided over by a Brigadier M.V. Wright of 7th Indian Brigade. A company of British
soldiers, armed with rifles and fixed bayonets, marched the accused men to and from the
courtroom four times a day. Some witnesses suspected every effort was being made to make
the soldiers appear to be dangerous criminals, instead of troops that had been badly let down
by their officers and army personnel administrators; troops who only a few months before their
arrest and trial had been fighting to restore democracy on the European continent.

There were a number of things that convinced the paratroopers their guilt had been
premeditated and their fate preconceived and decided, a factor which made legally defending
them virtually impossible – or so it was assumed by the court martial. However, Captain Reilly
entered a plea of 'not guilty' on behalf of all the men, and put forward a plea for condonation
by the military authorities.

After a short retirement to discuss the plea, the court martial was reconvened. It was then
announced it rejected the condonation plea. That decision to continue with the prosecution
of 13th Battalion, 6th Airborne Division on the charge of mutiny, when it reached Britain,
embittered the nation and brought scorn on the whole process of military courts martial.

However, the story of the paratroopers' strike didn't end there. That was mainly because
of the severity of the sentences that were imposed on the paratroopers. For after Captain
Reilly had made his closing speech, in which he declared 'I have never had the honour to
ask for mercy for more deserving men', the court martial, in its ultimate sadistic stupidity,
sentenced eight paratroopers to five years' hard labour; 235 paratroopers to three years' hard
labour; and only twelve of the paratroopers were found 'not guilty' and returned to their unit.

The British press and other media organisations had a field day reporting on the Malayan Mutiny. Questions relating to the court martial decision were asked in both the House of Commons and the House of Lords. Back bench MPs on both sides of the Commons, and on the opposition front bench, railed against the decisions as they related to the sentences imposed on 'the Red Devils', those 'fallen heroes'. It was certainly more than Winston Churchill, leader of His Majesty's opposition, could tolerate. He demanded to know why there had been many months of delay before the judge advocate had been invited to offer his legal opinion with regard to the sentences, what 'irregularities' there had been in the sentencing process and would the 'irregularities' have been exposed had there not been considerable public concern at the sentencing procedures and the reasons for the final results of the deliberations. Mr Churchill also emphasised that it was doubtful if this matter would ever have been exposed had it not received such widespread indignation from the general public through the medium of the national press. Bessie Braddock, the socialist Member of Parliament for Liverpool Exchange, said something like the following before the members of the House of Commons:

> It is a well known fact that a soldier has to do a job before he can complain, and then he is told after he has done the job there is no reason to complain. Therefore it would appear more sensible if soldiers were given instructions on how to complain, without them having to end up behind bars.

It has to be said, however, that the Malayan Mutiny had a marked effect on the disciplinary powers of future courts martial for all the British armed services, for under the Army Act of 1861, the punishment laid down for mutiny, or for failing when present to exert the utmost effort to suppress a mutiny, was death. There appears to have been no provision made under that Act for appeals against that sentence once it had been passed. That may have been the reason why other reported mutinous acts against authority were not tried by courts martial after the First World War, such as the Invergordon Mutiny of 1931 by men of the Royal Navy and Royal Marines, which was brought about by a reduction in armed services pay.

Mutiny within the armed services could be said to come about in two distinct forms: armed mutiny, as in the case of the naval mutiny on board HMS *Bounty* in 1789; or passive mutiny, as in the case of the paratroopers' strike at Muar Rest Camp, Malaya, in May 1946. Both these forms of mutiny were treated under the Army Act 1861 simply as mutiny – extenuating circumstances were not taken into consideration – and the penalty if found guilty in both cases was death.

The Malayan Mutiny, however, could be said to have highlighted the need for changes in the disciplinary procedures and laws, as they then existed within the armed services. New laws have now been introduced, not only for the three armed services but also for civilians employed by them in work operations overseas. The new laws also contain provisions for appeals against sentences, imposed by a court martial, and the Human Rights Act 1998 abolished the death penalty for air force offences and replaced that sentence with a maximum sentence of life imprisonment, as authorised by the Air Force Act 1955. The remaining provisions of the Act, which incorporated the European Convention of Human Rights into the law of the land, came into force in 2000.

An Obituary to a Working Man

Ernest Smith was born on 24 December 1925. His father, a veteran of the First World War, had obtained work in the docks during the Second World War, due to a labour shortage caused by the call up of young dockers and stevedores for military service. Mr Smith senior worked on in the port transport industry until his death; but it was through him that Ernest (and his brother Albert) obtained their 'dockers' briefs'. Ernest entered the port transport industry on 20 March 1950.

Ernest had attended White Hill School and Gordon Senior Boys' School, Gravesend, before the Second World War, and when the Prime Minister, Neville Chamberlain, declared war against Germany on 3 September 1939, Ernest was evacuated by sea on the Thames pleasure steamer *Royal Eagle*, to Dereham, Norfolk. However, on his fourteenth birthday he was returned to Gravesend to start work.

Before being called up for military service on 6 June 1944, Ernest was employed by Associated British Cinemas at the Majestic Cinema, Gravesend, as a commissionaire. After his war service with the Royal Navy and the 6th Airborne Division, which included involvement in the Malayan Mutiny of May 1945, Ernest worked as a registered dock worker for thirty-four years, until he took severance and found employment as a security officer with Associated Electrical Industries, at its Northfleet, Kent, factory, where he worked until his death from stomach cancer in June 1988, at the age of sixty-three.

Ernest Smith married Miss Joyce Barrow on 11 December 1948, soon after he was returned to the UK from Changi Military Prison in Malaya. Joyce survives him, as does a son and two daughters.

TALE 6

EXTRACTS FROM THE WARTIME AND POST-WAR SCRAPBOOK OF THE LATE CAPTAIN JAMES FRYER

Before I begin quoting extracts from Captain Fryer's scrapbook, perhaps I should explain who we Gravesenders, as we were more commonly known, are. We are river people, for the simple reason that we live near the banks of the River Thames. In the not too distant past, most Gravesend people earned their livelihoods from employments associated with working on the river, at sea or in factories whose raw materials were brought in or taken from them by lighters, Thames sailing barges or ships.

The jobs that were most important to we river people were as sea, river and dock pilots, Freemen-Watermen-Lightermen of the river, tugboat crewmen (more commonly known among the river fraternity as Tugees), merchant seamen, ship tug and barge repairers; or in the enclosed docks, on riverside wharves, or downriver in deep-water anchorages on the river as stevedores or dockers; or as shrimp fishermen.

Shrimp fishermen had for centuries sailed their small boats out of Boily Bay, a small inlet adjacent to St Andrew's church on the Gravesend waterfront, downriver towards the lower Thames, to fish for shrimp. That was in bygone days, before the polluted upper Thames water from London eventually permeated downriver to its estuary and decimated those small shellfish, or to be more specific, dwarf lobsters, almost to the point of extinction.

We people of Gravesend are West Kents, that is Kentish men, as opposed to the people who occupy the land east of the River Medway, who are the Men of Kent. Indigenous Kentish people are mainly descended from Saxons, who crossed the North Sea from the region of south Denmark and north Germany, in the fifth century AD, following the departure of the Roman legions.

The people of Kent were always a dour, obstinate lot, more especially when confronted with any form of invidious opposition. Their greatest strength, it could be argued in their favour, lay in their calm and resolute attitude to whatever trials and tribulations confronted them, as William the Conqueror discovered when he met a combined force of Kentish Men and Men of Kent at Swanscombe (a village some 20 miles east of London) soon after he had conquered

Shrimp boats at Boily Bay, Gravesend, 1930s. (Author's collection)

the rest of England in 1066. Having looked them over, he decided he didn't care to take them on in battle. So he wisely made a separate peace agreement with them – hence the county of Kent's insignia is *Invicta*, meaning 'unconquered'.

I don't intend to imply that there is a jingoistic attitude in Kentish people, for to be quite honest most of them have little or no knowledge of their own country's, let alone county's, history. But it has to be said in their defence that when the gauntlet has been cast down, they quickly become fully aware of their duties.

This tale, then, is the record, extracted from a battered old scrapbook, of one such Kentish man and of his heterogeneous crews of civilian tugboat men, who became welded together in mind and spirit, as did so many civilian tugboat crews during the Second World War. However, to be fair, it has to be pointed out that the captain came originally from the Isle of Sheppey, which means he was really a Man of Kent.

Jim Fryer, or to give him his full rank and name, Captain James Edwin Fryer DSC and Bar, was a tugboat captain employed, before the Second World War, by William Watkins Ship Towage (London) Limited.

Captain Fryer had a chequered career in the tugboat service, a career that began in 1920, when he joined William Watkins tug fleet, working on the River Thames out of Gravesend. He began work on the Thames serving first as a tugboat deckhand, before becoming a tugboat mate, then master. In 1935, for some petty misdemeanour, he was sacked by William Watkins, but reinstated in 1936 as 'watchman afloat'; then in 1938 he was promoted to 'storekeeper ashore', a job that was brought to an abrupt end in January 1940, when he was hastily sent back to sea, as master of the ST *Fair Play* 1, before being transferred to the ST *Foremost* 87.

Captain Jim Fryer on the bridge of *Empire Winnie*, Normandy, 1944. (By kind permission of Mr A.G. Fryer)

Captain Fryer was short and stocky, with bright blue eyes set in a round face. I must admit I never heard him laugh, but he seemed always to have a mischievous, impish smile, which was reflected in his eyes. He and his family moved from the Isle of Sheppey in the late 1930s in order that he and his sons, who either worked on tugs or came to work on tugs, could be closer to their place of employment at William Watkins' tugs office, the Sun Pier, Gravesend. So you may well ask: 'What was it that set Captain Fryer apart from other tugboat captains?' The answer to that question possibly lay in the fact he was in the right place at the right time. But nobody could say that his personal war service record was not exemplary. Let me enlighten you with extracts taken from remarks recorded aboard the ST *Foremost* 87, Registration No. 164503, for the month of May 1940. The scrapbook begins with a hastily written order (no date), addressed to:

The Master S.T. Foremost 87.
(Confidential)
You will take the Hull barges M.V Marjory H, and RO P. No.2 to Dunkirk. On arrival there you will take United Towage Company's gear off the barges, and apply to the Sea Transport

Damage to the tug *Arcadia* after she was attacked in the North Sea, 1941. (By kind permission of Mr A.G. Fryer)

A member of the tug *Empire Winnie*'s crew, Mulberry Harbour, June 1944. (By kind permission of Mr A.G. Fryer)

Officer who will hand over to you the F.23 for towing to Dover. Leave F. 23 there, and pick up barges Jean and R.O.P. No.5 and tow these to Calais, taking all towing bridles, shackles, etc off on completion, and proceed to Dover. All bridles, etc, of these four craft to be handed over to Sea Transport Officer on arrival at Dover, who is to forward same back to Hull by rail.

You will get your sheet instructions for Dunkirk at the Downs.

Wm. Cowperthwaite

Wednesday 22 May 1940:

Foremost 87: Lying in Dover harbour awaiting orders to proceed to sea. At 02.30a.m. Received orders by messenger from the King's Harbour Master, to stand by to proceed to Calais. At 08.30a.m. received official orders to steam direct to Calais, steamed clear of Dover harbour Eastern Entrance at 08.45a.m. arrived Calais harbour 11.00a.m. On arriving at Calais, I was ordered to force the lock gates, which had been bombed by German planes, causing them to be disabled. I managed to force gates back to lock-side after one and a half hours charging and steaming full ahead on engines. On doing this job I was ordered with all haste to get S.S. Katowice, which was loaded with refugees, and lying in the inner dock, from her berth and tow her out into Calais Roads, so that she could proceed to sea. While doing this job of work there was continuous air activity overhead, and also the harbour was being bombed. I took hold of S.S. Katowice at 12.45p.m., and finished with sailing her out of Calais at 14.00p.m., with the refugees cheering as she sailed away. Air raid still in progress when I returned to harbour, directly on re-entering Calais harbour I received orders to steam at once to the S.S. City of Christchurch, which had arrived in Calais Roads, and assist her from The Roads to Calais outer harbour jetty. Steamed out to S.S. City of Christchurch, which was accompanied by a British destroyer, and was being attacked by enemy aircraft. Took hold of the ship at 14.30p.m. And assisted her from Calais Roads to Calais dock. While assisting S.S. City of Christchurch from Calais Roads into Calais harbour, magnetic mines, three in number, exploded quite near. I managed to berth S.S. City of Christchurch undamaged, although the air raid was still in progress at 4.20p.m. I then received orders to steam to Calais Roads once again and assist M.S. Williamstown from Calais Roads to Calais harbour. Things a bit quieter now, but received orders to find out who and what M.S. Williamstown's sailing orders were, and her captains name, before assisting him into harbour. Carried this order through, then took hold of the same at 17.00p.m., and assisted M.S. Williamstown from Calais Roads to berth in the outer harbour. Finished at 19.00p.m., then made fast to quay – had tea in peace.

Thursday 23 May 1940:

Lying in Calais harbour standing by, two air raids between midnight and 01.40a.m. At 02.00a.m. I received orders to take hold of S.S. City of Christchurch. Took tow-ropes from ship's quarters, and was about to tow the ship away from quay, when I received orders to the effect that 5th Column Agents had given the order. Naval authorities detained two uniformed men in connection with these orders. S.T. Foremost 87 ordered to keep ropes on hook, in case of emergency. Stood by S.S. City of Christchurch till 14.30p.m. Then I was officially ordered to take hold of her and assist her from her berth to Calais Roads – air raid in progress. Finished seeing S.S. City of Christchurch clear of Calais Roads at 15.30p.m., then returned

SECRET SECTION I   Page 6

ORDER OF LEAVING ANCORAGE

COB I

G 3 (a) ✔ ALYNBANK   (504)
     (b) FLOWERGATE   (301)
          GEORGIOS P.   (331)
          PARKLAAN   (216)
          SIREHEI   (220)
          VINLAKE   (413)
          MODLIN   (218)
          SALTERSGATE   (407)

G 4 (a) ✔ MANCHESTER SPINNER (324)
          MARTIPOSA   (427)
     (b) BENDORAN   (426)
          PANOS   (205)
          VERA RADCLIFFE   (328)
          EMPIRE MOORHEN   (308)
          EMPIRE FLAMIGO   (306)
          EMPIRE BUNTING   (410)

G 5 (a) EMPIRE TAMAR   (611)
          EMPIRE TANA   (423)
          EMPIRE DEFIANCE   (512)
      ✗ FORBIN   (529)
          DOVER HILL   (502)
     (b) BECHEVILLE   (414)   } 2m

COB II

G 1 (a) GEORGE S. WASSON   (575)
     (b) BENJAMIN CONTEE   (558)
          WEST NOHNO   (353)
          MATT RANSON   (560)
          WEST CHESWALD   (364)
          ~~DAVID O. SAYLOR~~ ~~(573)~~
          ~~VITRUVIOUS~~   ~~(574)~~

G 2 (a) JAMES IREDELL   (559)
     (b) G.W. CHILDS   (577)
          JAMES W. MARSHALL   (552)
          GALVESTON   (456)
          POTTER   (465)
          WILSCOX   (463)
          BAIALOIDE   (570)
          ARTMAS WARD   (578)   } 3m

COB III

B R (a) ✔ LYNGHAUG   (121)
          NJEGOS   (215)
          WINHA   (222)
          AGIOS SPYRIDON   (230)
          INNERTON   (325)
     (b) ELSWICK PARK   (303)
          INGMAN   (117)
          EMPIRE WATERHEN   (409)
          BOLCIQUE   (419)
          ~~FORMIGNY~~   ~~(232)~~

A M (a) WEST HONAKER   (361)   NOTE
          AUDACIOUS   (555)   (a) Commodore's Ship.
          WEST GRAMA   (362)
          FLIGHT COMMAND   (267)   (b) Standby Ship for Commodore.
          VICTORY SWORD   (368)
     (b) COURAGEOUS   (657)
          OLAMBALA   (266)

The sailing order of block ships leaving anchorage in the UK for Normandy, June 1944. (By kind permission of Mr A.G. Fryer)

SECRET	**SECTION II**	**Page 6**

MASTHEAD HEIGHTS

SHIP	Height of Mast From Waterline
COB I	
331 (GEORGIOS P.)	
504 (ALYNBANK)	114 ft.
301 (FLOWERGATE)	
216 (PARKLAAN)	93 ft.
218 (MODLIN)	85 ft.
220 (SIREHEI)	
413 (VINLAKE)	64 ft.
407 (SALTERSGATE)	84 ft.
427 (MARTIPOSA)	87 ft.
324 (MANCHESTER SPINNER)	100 ft.
426 (BENDORAN)	95 ft.
205, (PANOS)	88 ft.
306 (EMPIRE FLAMIGO)	88 ft.
308 (EMPIRE MOORHEN)	70 ft.
328 (VERA RADCLIFFE)	100 ft.
440 (EMPIRE BUNTING)	98 ft.
423 (EMPIRE TANA)	105 ft.
611 (EMPIRE TAMAR)	135 ft.
414 (BECHEVILLE)	70 ft.
512 (EMPIRE DEFIANCE)	93 ft.
502 (DOVER HILL)	100 ft.
529 (FORBIN)	106 ft.
COB II	
353 (WEST NOHNO)	75 ft.
575 (GEORGE S. WASSON)	76 ft.
558 (BENJAMIN CONTEE)	81 ft.
560 (MATT RANSON)	81 ft.
573 (DAVID O. SAYLOR)	
364 (WEST CHESWALD)	84 ft.
574 (VITRUVIOUS)	
552 (J.W. MARSHALL)	80 ft.
559 (JAMES IREDELL)	80 ft.
577 (G.W. CHILDS)	85 ft.
456 (GALVESTON)	85 ft.
570 (BAIALOIDE)	90 ft.
465 (POTTER)	
463 (WILSCOX)	100 ft.
578 (ARTMAS WARD)	
COB III	
303 (ELSWICK PARK)	81 ft.
121 (LYNGHAUG)	90 ft.
361 (WEST HONAKER)	90 ft.
368 (VICTORY SWORD)	85 ft.
215 (NJEGOS)	105 ft.
232 (FORMIGNY)	
657 (COURAGEOUS)	86 ft.
362 (WEST GRAMA)	95 ft.
117 (INGMAN)	
409 (EMPIRE WATERHEN)	85 ft.
266 (OLAMBALA)	65 ft.
267 (FLIGHT COMMAND)	75 ft.
230 (AGIOS SPYRIDON)	60 ft.
419 (BOLCIQUE)	129 ft.
555 (AUDACIOUS)	100 ft.
325 (INNERTON)	84 ft.
222 (WINHA)	86 ft.

Block ships used in the construction of Mulberry Harbour, June 1944. (By kind permission of Mr A.G. Fryer)

THESE TUGS HELPED MAKE HISTORY . . .

"*On D-day, the synthetic harbours started moving, in pieces, across the hundred-odd miles of rough water to Normandy. This operation meant towing thirteen miles of piers, causeways and breakwaters, weighing in all over 1,000,000 tons. . . . The production in the United Kingdom of virtually all this artificial harbour equipment . . . was the most critical single project undertaken by Britain for the campaign in Europe.*"

(President Roosevelt.)

"*As a result of the skill of British experts, craftsmen and seamen, the Allied armies, with all their vital supplies, were put ashore in the most rapid military build-up in history, in spite of the worst June gale for forty years.* **The prefabricated ports made possible the liberation of Western Europe.**"   (Official Communique.)

Abeille VI	Empire Doris	Empire Larch	Gay Head
Abeille 20	Dundas	Lariat	Farallan
Abeille 21	Ebro	Lynch	Trinidad Head
Empire Aid	Eminent	Mammouth	Bodie Island
Algorma	Emphatic	Empire Meadow	Hillsboro Inlet
Allegiance	Emulous	Empire Nicholas	Moose Peak
Antic	Envoy	Owl	Sankety Head
Assiduous	Enticer	Partridge	Black Rock
ATR 4	Fairplay I	Empire Pixie	Great Isaac
ATR 13	Flaunt	Prizeman	Thames
ATR 54	Empire Folk	Queens Cross	Zwartzee
ATR 125	Freedom	Empire Race	ST 758
ATR 170	Goliath	Resolve	ST 759
ATR 172	Goole 10	Empire Roger	ST 760
Attentif	Griper	Empire Rupert	ST 761
Bandit	Growler	Sabine	ST 762
Empire Bascobel	Hudson	Samsonia	ST 763
Bat *Capt. J. Richardson*	Hesperia	Empire Sandy	ST 764
Empire Belle	Empire Harry	Empire Sara	ST 765
Empire Ben	Empire Henchman	Saucy	ST 766
Empire Betsy	Empire Humphrey	St. Martin	ST 767
Buccaneer	Empire Ivy	St. Mellons	ST 769
Champion	Empire Jane	Sea Giant	ST 770
Charing Cross	Empire Jester	Seaman	ST 771
Cherbourgeoise I	Empire John	Empire Seraph	ST 772
Cherbourgeoise III	Empire Jonathan	Sesame	ST 773
Cheerly	Empire Julia	Empire Silas	ST 774
Contest	Kewaydin	Empire Sinew	ST 780
Cormorant	Kings Cross	Stoke	ST 781
Danube VI	Krooman	Stormking	ST 782
Destiny	LT 22	Superman	ST 794
Dexterous	LT 130	Empire Vincent	
Director	LT 15	Empire Winnie	

A list of the tugs that took part in the Normandy invasion, June 1944. (By kind permission of Mr A.G. Fryer) to Calais harbour where I received instructions to proceed direct to Dover for provisions, coal and water. Arrived at Dover harbour 17.00p.m., and made fast at submarine dock.

Friday 24 May 1940:

Lying in Dover harbour's submarine basin. At 11.00p.m. received official orders to proceed to Calais harbour. Cleared eastern entrance of Dover harbour 11.10 and steamed for Calais. Arrived within one mile of Calais pier heads, heavy gun fire and bombing in progress, thought fit not to attempt to enter owing to bombarding; things looking very serious, several buildings ablaze. Stood by outside harbour for half an hour until advised by British destroyer to return to Dover. Headed for Dover harbour at 12.30a.m., arriving back at same 04.00a.m. Tug made fast inside submarine dock.

Thursday 30 May 1940:

Lying in Dover harbour awaiting orders. At 04.30a.m. received orders to accompany the Lady Brassy to Dunkirk. Steamed to Dunkirk arriving off beach at 14.30p.m. Heavy firing and shelling going on. Received orders to take barges Sark and Shetland in tow and beach them at Saint Malo, Dunkirk beach; barges Sark and Shetland then being at anchor half a mile to the east of Eastern Pier Heads, Dunkirk. Slipped anchors of barges Sark and Shetland, and under heavy barrage of gunfire, took same alongside S.T. Foremost 87. Then towed same to given position and beached them, finishing this job. It was very difficult owing to numerous wrecks in the vicinity, time 15.30p.m. I then received orders to enter Dunkirk harbour to render assistance wherever possible.

Heavy bombing and shelling going on everywhere, assisted transports to and from Eastern Arm of Dunkirk harbour, into Dunkirk Roads. Took hold of S.S. Prague at 21.00p.m., and assisted her from Eastern Arm Dunkirk, into Dunkirk Roads. Loud cheering going on, the troops pleased with themselves, heavy gun barrage beginning 21.15p.m. S.S. Prague now clearing Dunkirk, and steaming for home. At midnight, steamed ahead of British destroyer into Dunkirk harbour. It being very dark, with dense smoke from fires caused by shelling and bombing – assisted same to berth then stood by - things getting very uncomfortable.

Friday 31 May 1940:

Standing by in Dunkirk harbour, heavy barrage still in progress, shrapnel falling heavily on S.T. Foremost 87's deck. At 02.00a.m. received orders to proceed to Dover. Steamed out of Dunkirk harbour leading destroyer with S.T. Foremost 87. Cleared pier heads at 02.30a.m., and steamed to Dover, arriving in Dover harbour at 07.30a.m. Made tug fast in submarine basin at 7.45a.m. At 15.30p.m. I received orders to take sailing barges in tow – two in number – to Dunkirk, also to beach them on arrival at Saint Malo beach, Dunkirk. At 16.00p.m. took same in tow, and cleared Dover pier heads Eastern Dock at 16.40p.m., arriving in Dunkirk Roads at 21.50p.m. It was dark with dense smoke from fires, caused ashore by enemy bombing, with enemy aircraft overhead and heavy gun firing going on.

22.00p.m. I shortened the towropes, and hove the barges alongside S.T. Foremost 87. I then began to tow same towards given position to beach them. Carrying this job out under heavy gunfire, finished at 23.15p.m., and returned to Dunkirk harbour to render assistance wherever possible.

Saturday 1 June 1940:
Standing by in Dunkirk harbour, assisting wherever possible with destroyers and transports, at 03.00a.m. I received orders to return to Dover, arrived back in Dover at 07.00a.m.

Sunday 2 June 1940:
15.30p.m. Took lifeboats RLMB Cecil, Lillian, Philpot's, and Thomas Kirk Wright in tow, with orders to proceed to Dunkirk, and assist on arriving at same in evacuating troops, etc. Cleared Dover eastern pier head at 16.00p.m., and steamed towards given position arriving at about 21.40p.m. Gave lifeboat coxswain's [their] courses and position. Then when about to alter course for my given position, I noticed what proved to be the hospital ship Paris. On approaching her I witnessed several explosions and machine gunning. I also saw several lifeboats, with survivors from Paris, who had taken to the ship's lifeboats owing to being bombed and machine gunned, causing Paris to slowly fill with water. I at once gave orders [to my crew] for assistance to get survivors taken from these lifeboats, which were half-full of water. Managed to get 95 survivors in all from lifeboats – some seriously injured. Also took on board 13 Spaniards, who were in a lifeboat. I interviewed these, but could not get any satisfaction as to how they came to be adrift in a boat, so they were handed over to the army authorities on reaching Dover. Continued on journey to Dover when everybody was made as comfortable as possible at about 23.20p.m. And arrived at Dover pier heads Eastern Dock at 05.00a.m. One lad of 16 years passed away on board S.T. Foremost 87 at 02.00a.m. on 3rd June.

Landed all survivors at Admiralty Pier, Dover harbour – everything being ready to assist in getting wounded and others ashore as quickly as possible. Finished duty and made fast to Prince of Wales pier Dover at 06.30a.m.

At about 12.30p.m. a collision occurred between a destroyer and transport, the destroyer being loaded with British troops, some of who were thrown into the water – five in number. S.T. Foremost 87's crew managed to save three out of five – the others were picked up by a French motor launch. I landed these lads at Prince of Wales pier, where an ambulance was waiting to take them to hospital. Then made fast to pier at about 17.30p.m.

Monday 3 June 1940:
Lying in Dover harbour awaiting orders.

However 3 June 1940 shows a transpire certificate among the scrapbook papers, which was issued by Falmouth Customs and Excise office for ST *Foremost* 87 under the command of J. Fryer. The transpire was issued with a clearance under 'Destination–Sealed Orders'. The destination proved to be the evacuation of St Nazaire, western France, at the mouth of the River Loire. The date for the return from this expedition is shown as 16 June 1940.

On 20 June 1940 the following letter was received which read:

Captain J. Fryer,

Master S.T. Foremost 87.

I write on behalf of the government to convey to you, and the members of your ship's company, the gratitude and admiration felt for the help freely given and the courage and endurance displayed by you all in the evacuation from Dunkirk.

This operation, in which tugs and other units of the merchant navy joined as partners of the fighting services, was carried to a successful conclusion in the face of difficulties never experienced in the face of war.

I am proud to pay tribute to you, and that of your ship's company, in a great human adventure destined to occupy a place of honour in the pages of history,

Ronald Cross,

Minister of Shipping.

A letter from:

William Watkins Ltd,

Steam Tug Owners,

Fenton House,

112, Fenchurch Street,

London E.C.3.

19 August 1940.

Capt J. Fryer,

6 Jubilee Crescent, Gravesend, Kent.

Dear Captain Fryer,

DUNKIRK.

Your Directors wish to convey to you their hearty congratulations upon the award of the Distinguished Service Cross you received in the above operation.

Yours faithfully,

WILLIAM WATKINS LIMITED.

John R.W. Watkins, Director.

The crew of the ST *Foremost* during these precarious Calais and Dunkirk operations between 23 April and 19 May 1940 are listed as follows:

Fryer, J., Captain. 6 Jubilee Crescent, Gravesend.

Starkey, R.E., Mate. 62 Raphael Road, Gravesend.

Gibbens, W., Engineer. 17 Peacock Street, Gravesend.

Brignell, G., 2nd Engineer. Dungeness, Kent.

Lane, W.H., Deck Hand. 45 Peacock Street, Gravesend.

Watkins, T.G., Deck Hand. 55 Norfolk Road, Gravesend.

Garcia, L.J., Fireman. 1 Terrace Court, Gravesend.

Pictow, T.W., Fireman. The Terrace, Gravesend.

Onyett, J., Fireman. Coulthorpe Street, Gravesend.

Dire, C., Cook. 53 Alexandria Road, Gravesend.

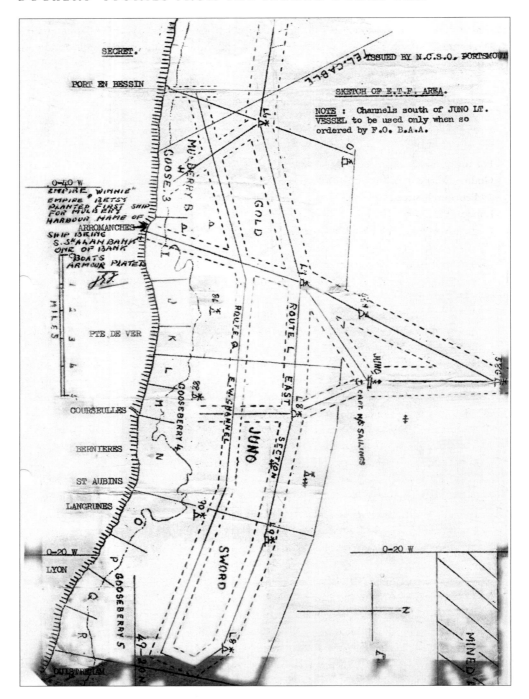

The invasion plan for landing British and Canadian troops on the beaches. (By kind permission of Mr A.G. Fryer)

The next incident in the scrapbook is a record of a salvage operation in the Thames estuary in December 1940. It is an operation that is recorded as follows, and which involved the ST *Arcadia*, No.105766 (call sign MQTJ), built 1895, gross tons 180.

S.S. Inginer N.Vlassopol.

STATEMENT
–of–
Capt J. Fryer, Master of the S.T. 'Arcadia'.

For and on behalf of:
Godfrey Warr & Co.,
19 Fenchurch Street,
London E.C.3.
James Edwin Fryer, 6 Jubilee Crescent, Gravesend, Kent,
STATES–

I am the master of the S.T. Arcadia, and have been master of that tug for the past two years. I have been in the employ of messrs William Watkins limited, the owners of Arcadia, for the past twenty-five years.

The Arcadia is a steam tug of some 180 tons register, her length is 109ft 1inch, her breadth 21ft 5 inches and her depth is 11ft. 8 inches. She is fitted with double expansion engines of 550 indicated horsepower.

The Arcadia is equipped with all necessary salvage plant, including a Merry Weather pump and necessary fire hoses, together with spare ropes, wires, anchors, etc., to enable her to perform all kinds of salvage work. She carries a crew of nine hands including myself: a mate, two deck hands, two engineers, two firemen and a boy cook.

At about 03.15a.m. on Saturday the 14th December 1940, I received orders to get under way for Gravesend. At that time I was moored at Trinity Quay in Harwich harbour waiting route instructions and orders to proceed. We cast off from the quay at 08.00a.m. And proceeded as ordered towards our destination, clearing the cork light vessel at 08.30a.m. The weather at this time was a very strong wind from the S.S.W., with a heavy sea and slight haze which only enabled my tug to steam at little over slow ahead on her engines, the flood tide (astern) enabling us to make about 6 knots.

On nearing No.9 buoy, barrow deeps, I observed the S.S. Inginer N.Vlassopol ashore between and inside Nos 9 and 11 barrow deep buoys. She was in a position aground on the west barrow sands heading in a westerly direction. I first observed the S.S. Inginer N.Vlassopol, when my tug was off about No.8 barrow buoy, at which time visibility was improving. As we proceeded I altered my course to approach the steamer's port bow. As we neared the S.S. Inginer N.Vlassopol, I observed another tug, the Sun V trying, to make fast [on her], but this was a very difficult job owing to the strong wind and heavy sea causing broken water around the ship.

As I neared the vessel the captain hailed me to take hold immediately. I then manoeuvred Arcadia into a position under the ship's port bow and, with great difficulty, managed to pass the end of my towing hawser on board. This consisted of 45 fathoms of 4inch towing wire and 90 fathoms of 12-inch manila towing rope. Thus altogether we had a scope of towrope and wire of approximately 135 fathoms.

I were made fast to the ship's port bow at about 12.30p.m. I then commenced to tow at full speed ahead on the engines towards deep water. We were towing at about a right angle off the ship's port bow, the other tug, Sun V, managed to connect her towing hawser at about 13.00p.m. We continued towing till about 14.30p.m., when I was instructed by the pilot, who had boarded the ship at 13.15p.m. to cease towing on this tide, as the water was falling, but to stand by the ship and take hold of her the next tide again from the port bow. My towing hawser was cast off from the ship at 02.45p.m. I then went to anchor in deep water abreast of the ship, and awaited the next flood tide as ordered. The weather was still very bad with a heavy sea running.

At 10.00p.m. we hove up the anchor, and steamed in towards the S.S. Inginer N. Vlassopol, whose crew were already mustered on the 'forecastle head,' ready to take the towing hawser, which was passed on board and made fast to the port bow. We were made fast at 10.15p.m. and commenced to tow at full speed as instructed by the pilot. We continued towing till about 12.30a.m. On Sunday 15th December when I were hailed by the master of the tug St.Clare, that was approaching our position at very slow speed, owing to the nature of the weather and poor visibility. I informed the Master of the St. Clare of our position and, on taking soundings, he steamed his tug towards the S.S. Inginer N. Vlassopol, connecting his towing hawser to the ship's port bow at 13.00p.m.

The tugs Arcadia and St. Clare were the only tugs engaged on this p.m. tide, the Sun V being at anchor on the other side of the channel, away from the ship. The Arcadia and St. Clare continued towing, till we were ordered to cast off hawsers, and take up the same positions for towage on the next tide, that being the a.m. tide on the 15th. The S.S. Inginer N. Vlassopol had been shifted slightly from her original position with the aid of the tugs Arcadia and St. Clare. Both tugs then went to anchor to wait for the a.m. tide.

At 10.15 a.m. on the 15th December, I steamed Arcadia towards the ship. The weather being foggy, with a visibility of about quarter of a mile, we again passed our towing hawser on board S.S. Inginer N. Vlassopol, being connected as before on the port bow. We were all fast at 10.30a.m., when we then commenced to tow at half speed, increasing the speed to full at 11.00a.m., as instructed by the pilot.

At 10.55a.m. the tug Sun VIII made fast to the port bow, as also were the tugs Sun V and the St Clare. Then all four tugs were ordered to tow in the same direction, away from the port bow.

At about 11.50a.m. the tug Badia was connected to the port bow, and the tug Persia to the starboard quarter. All tugs were then ordered to tow at full speed.

It was at about 12.20p.m. that I noticed the ship began to move towards deep water, and at 12.25p.m. the ship was towed safely away off the sands into deep water, in the fairway of the barrow deeps. All the tugs then cast off their hawsers from the ship at about 12.35p.m. Having hove Arcadia's towing hawser aboard, I went alongside with Arcadia and found the ship was safely anchored, but was unable to proceed owing to fog. The salvage officer, who had boarded the ship at about noon on Sunday the 15th, informed me he required me to stay in attendance with the ship, until she arrived off Gravesend. Badia was also requested to remain with Arcadia.

The Arcadia then made fast alongside the S.S. Inginer N. Vlassopol at 1.15p.m. (the fog having lifted a little) and the pilot informed me he was going to proceed and told me to keep

**Captain James Edwin Fryer
Distinguished Service Cross
and Bar**

CALAIS, DUNKIRK and ARROMANCHES

1940 - 1945

Right: Captain Jim Fryer DSC and Bar.
(By kind permission of Mr A.G. Fryer)

Below: Marconigram message received
by Captain Fryer from the Royal Naval
Officer in Command, Mulberry Harbour,
Arromanches, Normandy. (By kind
permission of Mr A.G. Fryer)

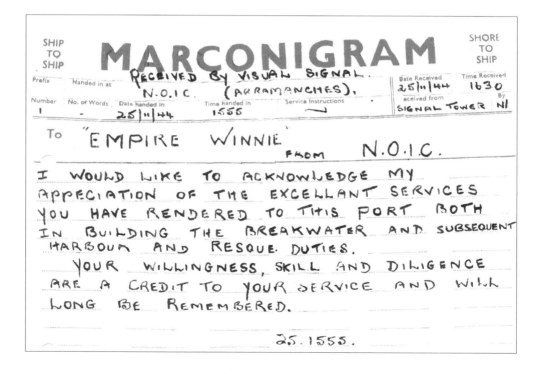

ST *Cervia*, later sunk off Tilbury Docks while towing the RMS *Arcadia* with the loss of six lives, 1952. (Author's collection)

in attendance. The Arcadia and Badia accompanied the ship until her arrival in Gravesend Reach at 18.00p.m. Where the S.S. Inginer N. Vlassopol was brought to a safe anchorage, in Higham Bight, Lower Gravesend Reach. As soon as the ship was safely anchored, I was informed my services were no longer required. I then went alongside the S.S. Inginer N. Vlassopol, and took the salvage officer on board Arcadia, and steamed to the S.S. King Lear, where I put the salvage officer aboard. I then steamed Arcadia to Terrace Pier, Gravesend, where I made fast at 19.00p.m.

At the time of my rendering Arcadia's service the S.S. Inginer N. Vlassopol, she was fully laden. She had a deck cargo, and was lying in a dangerous position.

Our services were performed in bad weather, and had it worsened, but for the services of the tugs employed, the S.S. Inginer N. Vlassopol could easily have damaged her rudderpost, and quite possibly have broken her back. The services of the tugs were the means of bringing the ship into a place of safety, due to their combined services, S.S. Inginer N. Vlassopol apparently sustained no serious damage.

James Fryer, Master of the S.T. Arcadia.

Captain Fryer's next direct contact with the enemy came on 12 April 1941, when in command of the ST *Arcadia*. Gravesend-based river tugs had for some time been employed as towing barges from the River Thames to Great Yarmouth. The barges were bound for Scotland but Great Yarmouth was used as a marshalling area, where tugs from Scotland took over the duties of towing the barges on to their Scottish destinations, via the Caledonian Canal.

ST *Empire Winnie*, Gravesend, 1946. (By kind permission of Mr A.G. Fryer)

On 12 April 1941, when she was just a few miles off the east coast port of Harwich, *Arcadia* was attacked by a German Luftwaffe Ju 88. The bomber aircraft dropped a stick of bombs, one of which passed through *Arcadia*'s funnel, fortunately without exploding. The plane then racked the tug with machine-gun fire. *Arcadia*'s crew fought back with whatever weapons were at hand (a .303 rifle), and the Ju 88 withdrew leaving *Arcadia* dead in the water, as the hole in her funnel resulted in the loss of draught, causing a reduction in steam pressure. *Arcadia* was towed into Harwich harbour, where emergency repairs were carried out.

The following letter was received by Captain Fryer:

William Watkins Ltd, Fenton House,
112 Fenchurch Street, London E.C 3.
9th May 1941.
My dear Fryer,

I am enclosing a copy of a letter received yesterday from Captain Sheffield, director of trade division admiralty, concerning your encounter with an enemy aircraft on 12th April last.

An oil tanker sunk by enemy bombs outside Mulberry Harbour, June 1944. (By kind permission of Mr A.G. Fryer)

A block ship used in building Mulberry Harbour, June 1944. (By kind permission of Mr A.G. Fryer)

I should also like to add my congratulations to you and your crew, for your determined efforts to bring this plane down, and I hope the next time you will have better luck.

Yours sincerely,

John R. Watkins, Director.

The crew of the ST *Arcadia* when this attack was carried out were:

Fryer, J., Captain. 6 Jubilee Crescent, Gravesend. Age 40.
Taylor, A., Mate. 176 Rochester Road, Gravesend. Age 35.

Wood, S., Able Seaman. 29 St James Road, Gravesend. Age 30.
Argent, R., Deck Hand. 54 Milton Road, Gravesend. Age 20.
Gibbons, W., Engineer. 17 Peacock Street, Gravesend. Age 37.
Merton, W., Engineer. 32 Hillside Avenue, Gravesend. Age 22.
Connelly, W., Fireman. 44 Prospect Place, Gravesend. Age 19.
Smith, P., Boy-Cook. 4 Dickens Road, Gravesend. Age 17.

Captain Fryer and his crew carried out numerous towing and salvage operations in all the war zones around the British Isles, Ireland, the North Atlantic and the Bay of Biscay, including the towage and placing of the Maunsell Sea Forts (the large reinforced concrete fortresses that were built at Red Lion Wharf, Northfleet, Kent, then floated downriver to their pre-designated sites in the Thames estuary), until he was called upon to take command of the newly launched ST *Empire Winnie* in 1944.

The ST *Empire Winnie* (No.169177, call sign MGRS) was built by Clelands (Successors) Ltd, of Willington Quay-on-Tyne. She was a large sea-going tug for her time, of 479 gross tons. When she went to sea, her crew was made up mostly of men from Gravesend; men who together with 129 other tugboat crews, drawn from British Commonwealth and Allied countries, aided the Royal Engineers of the British Army's transportation troops to create one of the most brilliantly contrived plans in military history, for the supply of equipment, ammunition and stores to the British and Canadian armies invading France (the American army had its own Mulberry Harbour), by the construction of an artificial prefabricated docking facility on the Normandy coast at Arromanches, better known under the code name of 'Mulberry'.

The Mulberry Harbour sections were secretly built at various locations along the River Thames, in dry docks within the enclosed London docks, and other sites around the British coast. The harbour's sections were constructed from concrete that was reinforced with steel and camouflaged by various means until required for 'Overlord' – the invasion of Normandy. It was then on D-Day minus one, 5 June 1944, that an armada of tugs descended on the many individual sections of the harbour and commenced towing them, together with block ships, across the English Channel, to be constructed together with the block ships into an invasion harbour: the Mulberry Harbour.

The recorded list for one formation of tugs to leave Oban, Scotland, under secret orders to fetch up off Arromanches was:

Tugs will leave as follows:-
'Empire Rupert' with Cob 1. 'Empire Larch' with Cob 2. 'Empire John' with Cob 2.
'Empire Winnie' with Cob 3. 'Empire Aid' with Cob 1.
When all are formed up, the Tugs will take station with Cob 1, as shown in formation diagram.

The crew of ST *Empire Winnie* during the construction of Mulberry Harbour were mainly men and boys from Gravesend. Their names listed in the tug's logbook at that time were:

Fryer J., Captain. Allen J., Mate. Tricky A.E., Lord N.J., Roach D., Macalister H., Raymond B., Howard R., Lea J., Cook W., Billham J., Bond J., Halfright G., Kimble W.R., Haydon H.J., Aves A., Westwach J.N., Whiffin R.W., Longman S.C., Harris T., Reynolds A.

The first block ship (SS *Alynbank*) to be sunk in position to begin the building of Mulberry Harbour was where Gold and Juno invasion beaches intersected off Arromanches. It was put in place by the steam tugs *Empire Winnie* under Captain J. Fryer, and *Empire Betsy* under Captain J. Woolnough.

The crew of *Empire Betsy* (No.180248, call sign MNNX), during this period of Mulberry's construction, are shown in the tug's logbook as being:

Woolnough J., Master. Sutherland J., Mate. Fryer J., Bos'n. The Able Seamen were: Kelly W., Smith J., Roots R. Engineer: Sonley G. Second Engineer: Potter T. Donkeyman: Roots J. Fireman: Bushell G., Wilson D. Cook-steward: Highway T.

Mulberry Harbour was, without doubt as extant records held by Mr. Frank R. Turner conclusively prove, the preconceived brainchild of Guy A. Maunsell, who submitted plans for the construction of such a harbour to the British Government in December 1940. The instigator of the 'concrete harbour' plan was a Lt Col Wilson, ADFW, War Office, a serving army officer, who asked Guy Maunsell to expand on an earlier idea utilising similar reinforced structures for the landing and supplying of troops operating in enemy territory.

The construction of sections of Mulberry Harbour was undertaken by a large number of companies on the Thames and around the British coast. When the time came, as early as May 1944, the concrete sections of this gigantic meccano set were towed from their construction sites, down rivers and the British coast, to assembly points ready to be picked up by the invasion's tug fleet and taken to the site off the Normandy coast at Arromanches, where they were then assembled.

On 25 July 1944, at 1630, a signal was received by Marconigram, addressed to:

'EMPIRE WINNIE'
From N.O.I.C. (ARROMANCHES).
I would like to acknowledge my appreciation of the excellent services you have rendered to this port, both in building the breakwater, and subsequent harbour and rescue duties.

Your willingness, skill, and diligence, are a credit to your service, and will long be remembered.
25. 1555.
                    BRITISH WIRELESS MARINE SERVICE.
On 4th August 1944 the following letter was sent out to all tugs involved in the Mulberry Harbour project:
Tug Control, Lee Tower, Lee-on-Solent, Hants.
To all Tugs:
Upon [my] turning over tug control to Captain W.P. Stocker RN, I send you deep appreciation for your fine efforts and [your] splendid accomplishments.

The most important contribution that you made to the success of the invasion, has now assumed historical importance.

I send you best thanks for a difficult task well done,
(Signed) Edmund J. Moan,
Captain U.S.N.R.

After aiding the Royal Engineers by sinking the block ships, and in assembling and placing the concrete caissons, a task that took several weeks, many of the tugs were withdrawn from the Mulberry Harbour project to carry out other towing and salvage operations. The following letter explains the value of *Empire Winnie's* involvement in the construction of Mulberry Harbour:

N.O.I.C. ARROW = S.N.O. DUNGENESS = S.N.O. SELSEY. A.N.C.X.F.
TUG CONTROL LEE = S.N.O. PEEL BANK
QUEEN OF KENT = FOSSBECK.
® C IN C. NORE = G IN C PORTSMOUTH.
SECRET:
With the completion of the piers at Arromanches, the evolution of building the harbour is concluded. Many of those that took part will be dispersing and taking up other duties.

I would therefore like to express my appreciation of the work of all those who have contributed to the building of a harbour the size of Dover, in a time that was never before thought possible.

It is still necessary that this harbour should be kept absolutely secret from the enemy, and therefore for some time yet your work must remain unknown and unreported.

The Senior Naval Officer in charge at Arromanches and his staff, have done a fine job of work, in a manner that is most creditable to all concerned. Only the bad weather prevented the whole project being completed in less than three weeks.

I would like to thank especially the tugs, under the able direction and administration of the tug control, Lee-on-Solent, Dutch, American and British alike, and whether army, navy or merchant service. Also the [men] handling the small craft on the near and far shores that have done so much towards the building of the harbour.

I am grateful also to the S.N.Os at Dungeness, Selsey and Peel Bank and their Staffs, for the good work they have done in assembling, preparing for sea, and sailing the equipment to the Far Shore, and I would congratulate the Staff of R.A.M.P. for their efficient planning and administration of the whole.

I shall be glad if Senior Officers will make my appreciation known to their subordinates.

201020B.

A letter dated 28 December 1944:
William Watkins Ltd, Steam Tug Owners,
'Fenton house' 112 Fenchurch Street,
London, E.C.3.
Ref: JRW/JPG
Dear Captain Fryer,

Having entered the sixth year of the war, and with the year 1945 about to break, I should like to take this opportunity to congratulate you and your crew on the fine work carried out since September 1939, but especially that performed from a few weeks before D-Day. Not only have you successfully carried out an exceptionally large amount of towage, and incidentally towed some very awkward objects under very trying conditions, but maintenance has also been kept at a high standard, despite long working hours.

I can assure you that your exertions have been watched with admiration by all concerned and you have enhanced the already high reputation of coasting 'tugees'.

In conclusion, I wish you a successful year in 1945, and hope it may see the cessation of hostilities,

Yours sincerely,

John R. Watkins (Director).

In Captain Fryer's case, his lot fell in January 1945 to assisting the Royal Navy by towing dummy submarines, built at Dundee, south. The following letter was received after one such venture:

A letter dated 14 February 1945:
William Watkins Ltd, Steam Tug Owners,
Fenton House,
112, Fenchurch Street,
London, E.C.3.
Dear Captain Fryer,

It gave me great pleasure when perusing 'The Times' to discover you have been awarded a Bar to your D.S.C., for services during the Liberation of Europe. None, I think, know better than I what you did and under what conditions.

Will you please accept my sincere congratulations on a well deserved decoration,

Yours sincerely,

John R. Watkins.

Principal Admiralty Overseer, Naval Officer in Charge,
Mathers Hotel, Dundee.
Date: 27th February 1945.   M.162/45.
To: Captain J.E. Fryer,
S.T. Empire Winnie,
C/o Messrs. Wm. Watkins Ltd.,
112, Fenchurch Street,
London E.C.3.
Dear Captain,

Many thanks indeed for your welcome letter dated 25th February, regarding towage of B.P.T. 40.

The points you mentioned are most interesting and will be of great value to me in making the reports desired by the Admiralty. One really good point is the fact that the target towed straight, which is clear proof the building of the Keel was true. It is often very easy in building to get the Keel off centre, and if the false bow is not dead true, the tow is often adversely

Tugs tied up on Gravesend Buoy off Sun Pier. (Author's collection)

Steam tug owned by Dicken–Page, 1960s. (Author's collection)

affected. We are preparing more for Ocean Towage, and I trust one day to have the pleasure of seeing you and your ship again.

Meanwhile many thanks for the interest you have had in the matter, and in sending you kindest regards, and all good luck for the future. Believe me to be,

Yours sincerely,

[Signature Unreadable]

Principal Admiralty Overseer.

A letter dated 3 March 1945:

House of Commons.

Dear Captain Fryer,

May I congratulate you upon your great distinction of being awarded a Bar to your D.S.C. I wish you the best of great fortune.

Lady Maitland joins me in kindest greetings to you and your family,

Yours very sincerely,

Adam Maitland.

Steam crane for loading or discharging heavy goods. (Author's collection)

A letter dated March 1945:
Ministry of War Transport,
Berkeley Square House,
Berkeley Square,
London, W.

Dear Captain Fryer,

I am glad to see your name included in the recent list of awards, which His Majesty has been pleased to approve in recognition of *outstanding service* during the invasion of Normandy.

I am familiar with your continuous good work throughout the War, and the circumstances under which you were awarded the Distinguished Service Cross in 1940. I congratulate you most heartily on your second decoration.

Yours sincerely,

R. Metcalfe

Director of Sea Transport.

To: Captain J.E. Fryer, D.S.C. tug 'Empire Winnie'.

With an end to hostilities tugboat crews returned to their normal duties, with the exception of those tugs employed in helping to salvage wrecks to clear the sea lanes in rivers and around the coast. In Captain Fryer's case he returned to Arromanches to raise the block ships that had helped to form Mulberry Harbour, and tow them to various destinations where they were cut up for scrap.

It was at this period *Empire Winnie* was transferred by the Government to the ownership of William Watkins Ltd, as a replacement for tugs lost by that company due to enemy action. *Empire Winnie* became *Zealander* and was quickly redeployed in the deep-sea towage operations of surplus landing craft to South America.

In 1948 Captain Fryer again found himself at odds with his employer, and was presented with a letter giving an outline of those jobs he had been employed in during his employment with that company, which is reproduced as shown below:

William Watkins Ltd,
Steam Tug Owners.
Fenton house,
112, Fenchurch Street,
London, E C.3.
11th November 1948. Ref: MH/ JPG.

TO WHO OR WHOM IT MAY CONCERN.

We certify the following to be a true record of *Mr. Fryer's* service with this company.

Joined	Left	Comments
26.06.20.	13.09.35.	Served as deckhand, mate and master on river tugs.
15.10.36.	28.05.38.	Watchman–afloat.
29.05 38.	05.01.40.	Storekeeper–ashore.
06.01.40.	09.05.42.	Master of tugs 'Fairplay 1' and 'Foremost 87,' on coastal

service. (During this time Mr. Fryer was awarded the D.S.C. for service rendered in the Dunkirk operation.)

10.05.42.	25.07.42.	Master of the river tug Arcadia.
06.03.44.	11.10.48.	Master of ocean going tug- 'Zealandia' ex 'Empire Winnie. Towing master outside Home Trade Limits. (Awarded bar to D.S.C. for Services rendered at Arromanches).

William Watkins Ltd.
Max Hamilton, Director.

A letter from the Admiralty dated 11 November 1948:
P.M. (Honours and Awards) Branch,

Admiralty,
Queen Anne's Mansions,
St. James's Park,
London, S.W.1.

With Reference to your letter of 8th November, which has been forwarded to me by the Secretary of the Central Chancery, and to the Distinguished Service Cross which is still outstanding, I write to inform you that the delay is very much regretted, but the decorations for 1945 are only now being received from the makers for general dispatch.

I wish to confirm however, that the Bar to the Distinguished Service Cross will be forwarded on to you as soon as it is available.

I am returning herewith the Admiralty letter notifying you of the award,

Yours faithfully,

T. Fisher White.

One of the final indignities to Captain James Edwin Fryer, a man who had given a lifetime of faithful service to his employer and courageous duty in war to his country, came from the most unlikely source. It was in an undated letter that came through the Royal Mail with the Bar to his DSC that read:

To Captain J.E. Fryer, D.S.C
BUCKINGHAM PALACE.
I greatly regret that I am unable to give you personally the Award which you have so well earned.
I now send it to you with my congratulations and my best wishes for your future happiness,
George R.I.

When Captain Fryer returned from his South American towage operations, he was given his pre-war job back as storekeeper ashore until his retirement. Once retired, Captain Fryer was awarded an ex-gratia pension by William Watkins Ltd, which was inadequate to meet his basic retirement needs. He applied for an incremental addition to his state pension, but was advised by a visiting DSS officer his income was just above the basic limit for entitlement. He therefore

Ocean trading ship loading with export cargo, London docks, 1960s. (Author's collection)

didn't qualify under existing DSS rules for an incremental supplement. To which the captain replied: 'Don't worry about it son. I've just not qualified for anything all my life.'

Captain Fryer then got a job as assistant part-time school caretaker at a local school, where he worked until his death on 27 September 1972, aged seventy-two.

As for his command tug during the Normandy landings and the installation of Mulberry Harbour, *Zealander* was sold to Adelaide SS Co. Ltd, of Adelaide, Australia, and cut up for scrap in 1974.

Guy A. Maunsell, the talented architect who devised and drew up the original plans for Mulberry Harbour, which were submitted to the British Government as early as December 1940, became a wealthy man but received no official recognition for his foresight and planning (see the booklet *The WW2 Forerunner to Mulberry Harbour*, published by Frank R. Turner, Glendale House), as well as for the Maunsell naval and army sea forts that were built to protect shipping in the Thames and Medway estuaries against infiltration attacks on shipping by E-boats and mine-laying by enemy aircraft.

On the other hand, Captain James Edwin Fryer received official recognition for his valiant wartime service in Calais Harbour; for conspicuous work during the evacuation of British and Allied troops from the Dunkirk beaches; for saving the lives of ninety-five survivors from the hospital ship *Paris*, which was being bombed and machine-gunned by enemy aircraft; for

Merchant ship after collision in the Thames. (Author's collection)

ship towage and difficult salvage operations in the River Thames and round the coast; and for the significant part he played in the construction of Mulberry Harbour during the invasion of Normandy. Those were the operations for which he was awarded a Distinguished Service Cross and Bar.

However it has to be admitted that it is doubtful if Captain Fryer, or any of his contemporaries for that matter, looked on those deeds as being anything other than part of a tug master's normal duties – yet when he died he had only a few pence left in his pocket. Obviously he could not have avoided doing the courageous things he did do, simply because he was that sort of man. But in all conscience I put it to you, the reader, is that the way a man who helped to create one of the greatest military engineering feats in the history of warfare, while working in collaboration with other tug masters and their crews, in conjunction with Royal Engineers of the British Army, in the construction of the Mulberry Harbour, should have been treated? However, British history shows that such treatment of its war heroes is nothing new, with the exception that is to those commanders and admirals in the upper echelons of the military: Marlborough, Nelson and Wellington. But I think I had best leave you, the reader, to be the arbitrator in any debate on that rather delicate subject.

TALE 7

MENTIONED IN DISPATCHES

It's quite odd how some small things bring to mind incidents that happened many years before, how the memory is suddenly jolted into recalling some incident that one had long thought forgotten, but such a jog to my memory occurred just recently, when I was talking to a lady artist, near the riverside ferry site on Gravesend's waterfront.

She was telling Iris, my wife, and I how she had moved to London from South Africa, but had then discovered Gravesend by the River Thames. She had fallen in love with the place because of all the different aspects of the river, which caught her artistic eye, such as the ships and barges; the light as it was reflected from the river's surface; the newly renovated Town Pier and of course the tug boats cruising back and forth with the tides, pulling container ships or passenger liners towards their allotted destinations; and of how she had moved to Gravesend so she could be close to the river. But, she said, she found it hard to get to know the elderly people of the town, who always appeared to hold her at a distance, how they were closed up and didn't communicate their feelings, or talk about their personal histories or backgrounds; and how she thought it may have been because she was a foreigner.

'No,' I told her. 'That's the way they are, or at least used to be.' Then I gave her a 'for instance' and told her the following tale:

Several years ago, some forty years after the Second World War had ended, I was sitting at my desk composing a letter to be sent to the Ministry of War Pensions in relation to a claim for a war disability pension for deafness by Tom, one of my brothers-in-law (I had six brothers-in-law once, but the reaper has been to visit five times, now I'm down to one), who had become exceedingly hard of hearing, and had to retire from work because of it. My sister Cathleen, whose husband he was, had told me he had been deafened by bomb-blast while serving with the Royal Air Force in Trincomalee, Sri Lanka, when a Japanese battle fleet had closed on the island and sent aircraft carrier-borne planes to bomb the British naval base and airfield there in 1942.

It was while I was employed in this exercise that my eldest sister Violet and her husband Robert (known universally among the river fraternity as Bob) turned up to visit, and, being a bit on the nosey side, she asked me what I was doing. When I explained I was applying for a war pension for her brother-in law, she nodded at her husbband and said: 'I don't know why he doesn't apply for a war pension too. He's as deaf as a wooden post.'

Captain Robert (Bob) Fuller and Violet Fuller. (By kind permission of Mrs Diana Newman – daughter)

'What's that you say?' He barked at her.

'I said you're deaf, you silly old sot,' she shouted back at him. 'Turn that damn hearing aid on.'

He quickly did as she ordered; well that's how it was in their house - he was a ship's captain when he was at sea but reverted to first mate when he got back home. Then I said to him, 'Vi says you should apply for a war disability pension, because you're deaf. I've never known it when you weren't deaf. Tom was deafened by bomb blast. What's your excuse?'

'It was that bloody *Warspite*.' HMS *Warspite* was an old British battleship, a naval relic left over from the First World War that was armed with 16in guns that now repose outside the Imperial War Museum, London.

'What had the *Warspite* to do with you being deaf?' I asked him.

'Well, the bloody thing opened fire on the German gun positions when we were still close to the beach,' he said.

'The beach! What beach are you talking about? Margate beach?!'

Thames sailing barge under full sail. (Author's collection)

'No, you cheeky young sot, the Normandy beach at Arromanches,' he barked at me as though I should have known what he meant.

'When was this?' I had the impertinence to ask.

'On D-Day. You know… the day we invaded Normandy.'

'We invaded Normandy? Where did you get the "we" from?'

'No, not you, you silly blighter. You was too young. When I say "we" I mean the Royal and Merchant Navies and the British and Canadian armies.'

'Weren't the Americans there, too?' I said taunting him.

'No, they bloody well were not. They landed on the Cherbourg peninsula, on beaches code-named Omaha and Utah. The British and Canadians with contingents of Free French, Polish, and other Allied troops, were landed on Gold, Juno and Sword beaches.'

'So what were you doing on D-Day in your tugboat, while the troops were landing?'

'There weren't any troops landing when we got there. I was on a tug called the *Empire Pixie*, and we were towing Thames lighters, filled with ballast, that were to be beached to form a breakwater for the infantry carrying landing craft. On top of the ballast, in the lighters, were Royal Marine Commandos who, as soon as we ran the lighters ashore, leapt off the lighters and disappeared inland. The last part of our job was over, but those poor bloody commandos' jobs were just about to begin. I had steered the *Pixie* and the lighters as close in to the shore as I could, before the commandos got off, so as to give the lads a better chance of getting over the beach alive, because by this time all hell had been let loose.'

'Now that was very laudable of you,' I told him. 'but how did that cause your deafness?'

'What's that? What's that you say?' he replied.

'Never mind,' I half shouted back at him. 'What happened next?'

'Well, before we had time to get out of the way, that bloody HMS *Warspite*, and its grey-funnelled escorts, opened up on the German gun positions ashore. The *Empire Pixie* and the other tugs that had taken the lighters into the shore were ordered to get out of the way or get blown out of the water. What with the damn woof-woof of the guns, the soddin' whiz-whiz as the shells passed overhead, and the crash-bang-wallop when the bloody shells landed, by the time our tug had cleared the beaches, and got behind the British fleet on our way back to England, the whole of the *Pixie*'s crew were sticking their fingers in their ears, and shaking their heads, trying to hear each other when they spoke.'

'That story is a bit stretched out, isn't it,' I said. 'So what happened then?'

'He got a letter and a medal with three Oak Leaves,' said Vi. 'Show Henry the letter.'

Bob opened up his weather-beaten old wallet that was full of scraps of bits of paper, and selected one piece that had a hole in the centre, where it had been worn away over many years by the folds. It obviously hadn't seen the light of day for years and would have blinked had it have had eyes. On that dilapidated old worn out scrap of paper was printed:

By the KING'S Order the name of Seaman Robert Fuller,
Merchant Navy S.T. Empire Pixie,
As published in the London Gazette on 23rd January 1945,
As mentioned in a Dispatch for Distinguished Service,
I am charged to record His Majesty's high appreciation.

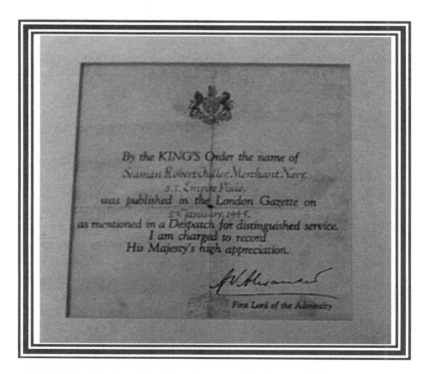

A copy of Bob Fuller's Waterman and Lighterman's certificate. (By kind permission of Mrs Diana Newman)

Bob Fuller's Mentioned in Dispatches award, for bravery, skill and courage on the beaches of Normandy, D-Day 1944. (By kind permission of Mrs Diana Newman)

MV *Brentwood* captained by Robert (Bob) Fuller. A post-war photograph. (By kind permission of Mrs Diana Newman)

Mentioned in Despatches.
Seaman Robert Fuller,
Merchant Navy of Gravesend,
Has been mentioned in despatches
For courage, determination, and skill,
During the landing of Allied Forces
On the Coast of Normandy.
I took hold of the document, and told Bob I would get it repaired, and framed. I would also send away for his other war medals, which, up to that time, he had never bothered to claim. I also wrote to the Ministry of Pensions on his behalf, claiming a war disability pension.

'Now I want you to grasp this situation,' I emphasised to the lady artist. 'My brother-in-law, Bob Fuller, before his retirement had been the captain of petrol and oil tankers which plied their trade between the River Thames and various ports round the British coast, on the continent of Europe from France, Belgium, Germany and Holland. Bob knew the coastal sea routes and river fairways in all those places better than he knew the proverbial back of his calloused, weather-beaten hands. However, when a Ministry of Pensions letter came, with a railway travel warrant, requesting he should attend Charing Cross Hospital in London for the audible testing of his ears, he arrived in London and went down into an underground station. And can you believe this,' I told the lady artist. 'He got himself lost on the underground railway.'

Cargo vessel, River Thames, 1960s. (Author's collection)

Addendum

The Fullers were a family of Freemen-Watermen-Lightermen of the River Thames. They were quiet men, excepting when they had a flare-up of bad temper. Otherwise they were not given to using too much rhetoric. During the First World War, Bob Fuller's eldest brother William was awarded his war medals by King George V, at the age of eleven, having served as the mate on his father's barge, which sailed war supplies to the British Army in Belgium and France.

During the Second World War, Bob's father, who was captain of the ST *Lion*, and one of his brothers, were lost when the *Lion* was sunk by a mine in the River Medway estuary, two and a half cables from number 5 Medway buoy, on 6 January 1941. (There were twelve boats reported lost to enemy mines in the Thames and Medway estuaries between December 1940 and January 1941.)

There are two unkempt war graves in St James' village churchyard on the Isle-of-Grain, Kent. One is that of an unknown Royal Air Force sergeant; the other is of an unknown merchant seaman. It was always Bob's opinion that the merchant seaman's grave is his father's. Bob died on 19 October 2000 and his ashes were put with those of his wife Violet, in St Mary's churchyard at Chalk, near Gravesend, our parish church. Each time I drive past that holy place, I'm sure I can hear her voice nagging at him: 'You may be the bloody ship's captain when you're aboard your boat, but you're only the soddin' mate when you're home here – turn that damn hearing aid on.' Then hearing his rasping reply, 'What's that you say? What's that?'

A merchant vessel after a collision in the Thames Estuary. (Author's collection)

P&O liner *Strathnaver* outward bound from Tilbury, Essex. (Author's collection)

ST *Empire Pixie*

The *Empire Pixie* wasn't a unique vessel: she was one of a number of 'Warrior class' tugs that were hurriedly built and launched to replace those many tugs lost to enemy action during the early years of the Second World War. They were designed as expendable tools, to be used in future operations at sea, of which the D-Day landings and the installation of Mulberry Harbour are just two incidents.

The *Empire Pixie* (Registered No. 168790, Yard No. 376) was launched on 5 November 1942. She was of a medium size, being some 263 gross tons with a length of 109ft 9in, a beam of 26ft 1in, and she drew 12ft 6in of water when afloat. It is recorded that until 28 March 1944 she was employed on naval duties. From that date there is no record of her activities until D-Day 1944, when it is recorded that Robert Fuller, merchant seaman of Gravesend, was 'Mentioned in Dispatches'.

Merchant vessel outward bound off Gravesend. (Author's collection)

Tugs awaiting sailing orders, Sun Pier, Gravesend. (Author's collection)

However, what was unusual in the make-up of the *Empire Pixie*'s crew was the age disparity between the men and the fact they were mostly men from North and South Shields. They are listed in the tug's log for 1943–44 as being:

Captain Robert Claspen. 21 Trojan Street, South Shields. Age 52.
Mate R. Burdey. 14 Sibthorpe Street, North Shields. Age 59.
Helmsman Robert Fuller. Old Road East, Gravesend, Kent. Age 23.
Able Seaman Robert Rogers. 92 Coltridge Avenue, South Shields. Age 26.
Able Seaman Stanley Dryden. South Eldon Street, South Shields. Age 22.
Able Seaman William Macloud. Kindebig, Tarlent, Harris. Age 31.
Able Seaman James Murray. 5 East Carlton Terrace, Buckie. Age 66.
Chief Engineer John Emmerson. 175 Trevor Terrace, North Shields. Age 61.
Technical Engineer Charles Lee. 51 Edith Street, South Shields. Age 59.
Fireman Jack T. Reed. 6 Brockley Street, South Shields. Age 53.
Fireman John Delaney. 14 Newflats, Greens Place, South Shields. Age 59.
Fireman George Stoker. 22 Slait Street, South Shields. Age 33.
Cook Thomas E. Howard. 4 Providence Grove, Hull. Age 35.
Cook Roy Rogers. 92 Coleridge Avenue, South Shields. Age 27.
Gunner Roy Bottomley. 43 Westborough Drive, Halifax. Age 20.

It has to be recorded, therefore, that if Walmington on Sea produced the men that formed the fictional 'Dad's Army' of the 'Home Guard', then North and South Shields most certainly must be among the top claimants to have produced the 'real' seamen for 'Dad's Merchant Navy' of the Second World War. Yet I very much doubt if either town has ever heard of the *Empire Pixie*, or of the bravery of the 'old fellows' of those two towns that served in her.

Other titles published by The History Press

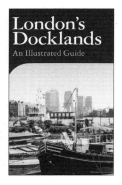

London's Docklands: An Illustrated Guide
GEOFF MARSHALL

The Port of London has changed beyond all recognition in the past four decades. Once the docks teemed with men and ships from all over the world, now all is transformed and a new and vibrant area has grown up with commerce, stylish housing, fashionable shops and restaurants.

    The author takes the reader on a journey. He outlines the historical development of the area from Roman beginnings and the Elizabethan Legal Quays to the construction of the largest system of docks in the world. Life in the docks is described, their eventual demise and the rebirth of Docklands with the development of Canary Wharf. There follow ten walking tours giving the reader an insight into the history, architecture and traditions of Docklands from Tower Bridge to the Royal Docks and Bermondsey and Rotherhithe.

978 0 7524 4221 1

Submariners' News: The Peculiar Press of the Underwater Mariner
KEITH HALL

For many years submariners produced 'local newspapers', reporting from the deep with a unique take on their unusual lifestyle. Held in much affection by submarine crews, they enjoyed a long period of popularity from the 1970s–1990s for their irreverent and decidedly un-PC approach to underwater life.

    In this funny book, author Keith Hall examines the development of this strange branch of 'underwater journalism', collating the articles and anecdotes, jokes cartoons and stories that have been published over the years to brighten up the lives of submariners far from home, providing an insight into the bizarre self-contained world of the submariner.

978 0 7524 5793 2

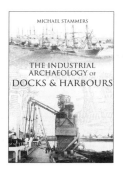

The Industrial Archaeology of Docks & Harbours
MICHAEL STAMMERS

Michael Stammers tells the history of the British harbour and looks at the industrial archaeology of both harbours and ports. For over 2,000 years, we have built man-made harbours and, as an island nation, they have played a great part in our history. From the smallest harbour to huge 'super ports' like Southampton and Felixstowe, every harbour or port can give a clue to its history and development and Michael Stammers takes us through the history and shows us what remains today to give a clue as to the history of the ports.

978 0 7524 3900 6

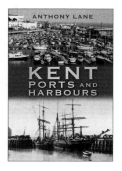

Kent Ports and Harbours
ANTHONY LANE

Kent Ports and Harbours charts the changes that have occurred over the last 400 years to the Kent ports and their associated shipping industries. It covers the development from naval dockyard to commercial port that took place at Chatham and Sheerness, along with the growth of the well-known seaside towns such as Margate and Ramsgate which expanded as the paddle steamers reduced the dangers of sea travel. Starting with the sailing vessels fishing or carrying small cargoes and finishing with the modern ferries, tankers, car carriers and container ships of today, this highly illustrated book emphasises the variety of seafarers, craft and harbour environments that can be found in Kent waters.

978 0 7524 5363 7

Visit our website and discover thousands of other History Press books.

www.thehistorypress.co.uk